ASSET
PROTECTION

for Business Owners and High-Income Earners:

How to Protect What You Own From Lawsuits and Creditors

D1416016

By Alan Northcott

Asset Protection for Business Owners and High-Income Earners: How to Protect What You Own From Lawsuits and Creditors

Copyright © 2009 by Atlantic Publishing Group, Inc.

1405 SW 6th Ave. • Ocala, Florida 34471 • 800-814-1132 • 352-622-1875–Fax

Web site: www.atlantic-pub.com • E-mail: sales@atlantic-pub.com

SAN Number: 268-1250

ISBN-13: 978-1-60138-005-0   ISBN-10: 1-60138-005-4

Library of Congress Cataloging-in-Publication Data

Northcott, Alan, 1951-
  Asset protection for business owners and high income earners : how to protect what you own from lawsuits and creditors / by Alan Northcott.
      p. cm.
  Includes bibliographical references and index.
  ISBN-13: 978-1-60138-005-0 (alk. paper)
  ISBN-10: 1-60138-005-4 (alk. paper)
  1. Executions (Law)--United States--Popular works. 2. Debtor and creditor--United States--Popular works. 3. Fraudulent conveyances--United States--Popular works. I. Title.
  KF9025.N67 2009
  346.7307'7--dc22
                              2008052660

Printed in the United States

STAFF BOOKS MANAGER: Melissa Peterson • mpeterson@atlantic-pub.com
INTERIOR DESIGNER: Nicole Deck • ndeck@atlantic-pub.com
COVER DESIGNER: Jackie Miller • sullmill@charter.net

We recently lost our beloved pet "Bear," who was not only our best and dearest friend but also the "Vice President of Sunshine" here at Atlantic Publishing. He did not receive a salary but worked tirelessly 24 hours a day to please his parents. Bear was a rescue dog that turned around and showered myself, my wife Sherri, his grandparents Jean, Bob and Nancy and every person and animal he met (maybe not rabbits) with friendship and love. He made a lot of people smile every day.

We wanted you to know that a portion of the profits of this book will be donated to The Humane Society of the United States. *–Douglas & Sherri Brown*

The human-animal bond is as old as human history. We cherish our animal companions for their unconditional affection and acceptance. We feel a thrill when we glimpse wild creatures in their natural habitat or in our own backyard.

Unfortunately, the human-animal bond has at times been weakened. Humans have exploited some animal species to the point of extinction.

The Humane Society of the United States makes a difference in the lives of animals here at home and worldwide. The HSUS is dedicated to creating a world where our relationship with animals is guided by compassion. We seek a truly humane society in which animals are respected for their intrinsic value, and where the human-animal bond is strong.

Want to help animals? We have plenty of suggestions. Adopt a pet from a local shelter, join The Humane Society and be a part of our work to help companion animals and wildlife. You will be funding our educational, legislative, investigative and outreach projects in the U.S. and across the globe.

Or perhaps you'd like to make a memorial donation in honor of a pet, friend or relative? You can through our Kindred Spirits program. And if you'd like to contribute in a more structured way, our Planned Giving Office has suggestions about estate planning, annuities, and even gifts of stock that avoid capital gains taxes.

Maybe you have land that you would like to preserve as a lasting habitat for wildlife. Our Wildlife Land Trust can help you. Perhaps the land you want to share is a backyard— that's enough. Our Urban Wildlife Sanctuary Program will show you how to create a habitat for your wild neighbors.

So you see, it's easy to help animals. And The HSUS is here to help.

THE HUMANE SOCIETY OF THE UNITED STATES.

2100 L Street NW • Washington, DC 20037 • 202-452-1100
www.hsus.org

Dedication

To my wife Liz—
long may we continue
to adventure together through life!

Table of Contents

Foreword

The area of the law known as asset protection has been receiving a great deal of publicity in recent months. As real estate prices drop and the economy falters, both wealthy and average Americans realize that their assets are exposed not only to the risks of the day-to-day market forces, but also to the risk of seizure by creditors. In a down economy, this risk of seizure becomes much more pronounced.

As real estate investors and business owners experience significant slow-downs in their businesses, they become unable to perform on their loans and leases. In many cases, a default on the loan allows the lender to seek a deficiency judgment or to pursue the borrower on a personal guaranty. This places all assets owned by the borrower at risk.

If the economy was not bad enough, our daily activities expose our assets to great risks. Parents with teenage kids who drive find out that the kids can be a great source of liability exposure. A surgeon may find that his malpractice coverage will not cover all claims. A widow may find that the inheritance she received from her husband is sought by his creditors. A business owner may be sued by his employees or customers. Both life and business are full of risk. If the risk results in a claim and a subsequent legal judgment, the plaintiff becomes your creditor. He can now use that judgment to seize your assets. Everything you have worked for your entire life can be lost in one swoop. Fortunately, it is easy to protect your assets from the risks we all face.

There is no "silver bullet" structure in asset protection planning. Attorneys pick from dozens of available structures, based on your risk exposure, your risk tolerance, the types of assets you own, and the aggressiveness of your likely creditor. The dozens of structures at play have one thing in common. They all transfer assets out of your name.

Limited liability companies, limited partnerships, irrevocable trusts and post-nuptial agreements are all examples of commonly-used asset protection techniques. These structures are straightforward, usually tax neutral and effective. All that they require is willingness to act and access to good advice.

Alan Northcott's *Asset Protection for Business Owners and High-Income Earners: How to Protect What You Own from Lawsuits and Creditors* is a great place to get such advice.

The book is well-written and the frequent use of case histories allows the reader to connect on a more personal level. It covers all of the frequently-used asset protection strategies in a form that is easy to understand. Complex legal theories are broken down, explained, and translated into practical uses. The reader comes away with a feeling of having acquired useful, practical knowledge.

The book is not aimed at attorneys, but at every American with assets to protect. You will learn the many options that you have to protect your residence, rental real estate, business, bank account, investment account, retirement plan, collectibles, and other assets that you value.

If you have assets, there is always someone who wants to take them from you. Read this book to learn what you can do to keep your assets.

—Jacob Stein, ESQ.

Mr. Jacob Stein is a partner with the law firm Klueger and Stein, LLP, in Los Angeles, California. The firm's practice is limited to asset protection, domestic and international tax planning, and structuring complex business transactions. The firm's goal is to provide the highest quality legal work that is usually associated with only the biggest law firms, in a boutique firm setting.

Stein received his law degree from the University of Southern California, and his Master's of Law in Taxation from Georgetown University. Stein has been accredited by the State Bar of California as a Certified Tax Law Specialist and is AV-rated (highest possible rating) by Martindale-Hubbell.

In the arena of asset protection Stein assists high net-worth individuals and successful businesses in protecting their assets from plaintiffs and creditors by focusing on properly structuring asset ownership and business structures and operations. Over the course of his career, Stein has represented hundreds of clients, including: officers and directors of Fortune 1000 companies; celebrities; Internet entrepreneurs; real estate developers, builders and investors; physicians; small business owners; attorneys, accountants and financial advisors; and many other individuals facing the adversity of a lawsuit.

Klueger & Stein, LLP
16000 Ventura Boulevard, Suite 1000
Encino, California 91436
Tel. 818-933-3838 • Fax 818-933-3839
e-mail: jacob@lataxlawyers.com
www.lataxlawyers.com
www.maximumassetprotection.com

Introduction

Congratulations, by picking up this book you have taken the first step in ensuring that what you have worked so hard to achieve is not taken away from you. Although this book is directed at small business owners and wealthy people, I believe that everyone can learn something of value from studying it. It is not just those people who think of themselves as rich who need to plan for unsavory eventualities — if you own much of value, you can easily become a target for unscrupulous lawyers and fraudulent claims that will rapidly deplete your resources. It is unfortunate that we live in such a world, but there are steps you can take to legally shield yourself and preserve what wealth you have.

Before we dive into the ever-changing world of asset protection for insulating yourself from lawsuits, you should ask yourself a few questions. The first question is: does worrying about protecting your assets keep you awake at night? In any case, how confident are you that your investments are positioned properly? With the turbulent times we are facing in our economy, it is more important than ever to protect your assets. If you are a business owner or a high-income individual, you are already an obvious target for lawsuits and a contested divorce could decimate your assets.

People choose to invest their money in many ways. Some will rely on the stock market or bonds and mutual funds. Those who can are well advised to invest the maximum possible in 401K plans. Many people buy real estate, sometimes for weekend and vacation homes, and sometimes because of the rental market, with the expectation that the value will grow over time. Others find comfort in investing in gold and other precious metals, or in collectables, to have something that is more tangible than pieces of paper.

Often, you will have started accumulating wealth with little thought to how to protect it in the future. Perhaps, if you have rental real estate, you have purchased landlords insurance and been advised that you are covered against being sued for common mishaps by your tenant. This is far from the case, and you need to be cognizant that insurance is seldom the complete solution, although it does have a place in your planning.

No matter where you are in your career and wealth creation plan, you need to read and assimilate the information in this book, and, most importantly, start right now by creating a plan to surround yourself with the appropriate elements to protect your lifestyle. There is no telling when you might become a target of a lawsuit, even a mischievous and unfounded one, and if you wait until then, you will find it much more difficult to preserve what is yours. Actually, there are laws that will work against you if you try to save your assets after a lawsuit has been filed.

In this book, I will run through the reasons for protecting your assets and the threats that you should be aware of. Asset protection is not just about avoiding unnecessary lawsuits, but also includes tax implications and avoidance, as the tax man taking your assets is just as real a threat. This applies particularly in the realm of inheritance tax. While you may no longer be actively involved when you are dead, you would probably wish to leave as much of your estate as possible to your family and friends rather than the government.

In this book, more detail is provided about the various scenarios and problems that you may face. According to Arnold S. Goldstein, Ph.D., in his book So Sue Me! "You have one chance in five that you will be sued next year," so complacency is not an option. When you are in that situation, it is normally too late to do anything about it, so planning ahead is one point that is emphasized. The government and state do provide some exemptions, but these are commonly woefully inadequate in protecting your main resources and income.

If you are a hardworking and resourceful entrepreneur and have your own business, you have particular problems — whether being sued personally can impact your business, whether your business being sued can impact your personal effects, and also the best ways to get around any detrimental issues. It is not just the business being sued by a client or injured bystander; you can also suffer from employees' actions, or even the actions of a partner. Do not worry; there are ways to structure your organization to provide a shield from these. A corporation that is registered in Nevada does not provide you with unlimited benefits, contrary to what you may be told by some seminar presenters who present it as the answer to all your concerns.

Arnold S. Goldstein handles all aspects of asset protection, and is recognized as an expert in the field.

SUCCESS STORY: ARNOLD S. GOLDSTEIN

Arnold S. Goldstein, Ph.D., best-selling author and attorney, has protected the assets of thousands of individuals and companies nationwide. A popular radio and television guest, he has appeared on CNN, CNBC, and the Today Show. His wealth protection strategies have been featured in Inc, CFO, Business Week, Entrepreneur, Success, Forbes, Fortune, and in other major publications. He lives in Delray Beach, Florida.

For more information, visit his Web site: **www.asgoldstein.com**, or call (561) 953-1050 or 1-800-887-0748

In what way are you involved with asset protection, and does this include general estate planning, such as for tax issues?

My firm handles all aspects of asset protection including the formation of entities, both domestic and foreign, transfers into entities, preparation of operating agreements, strategic planning for clients to protect all their different types of assets. We work with the client's accountants and financial planners to best serve the client's asset protection needs. We integrate the asset protection plan with the client's existing estate plan or prepare the estate planning documents ourselves. We deal with estate tax savings issues but no other tax issues.

SUCCESS STORY: ARNOLD S. GOLDSTEIN

Do you specialize in any particular aspects of asset protection, such as foreign trusts or LLCs?

I do not specifically specialize in any particular area of asset protection as each client's needs are different. I provide a comprehensive plan to my clients that can include any number of entities and trusts, whichever are needed by the client.

In your experience, do you find that a single entity or strategy is sufficient for most people, or do you commonly recommend a multi-layered structure?

Whether or not to provide a client with a single entity or a multi-layered plan depends on what type of assets the client needs to protect and how title is held. In addition, I examine who the participants are and how everything needs to be tied to their estate plan (i.e. using a family limited partnership to reduce estate taxes). All plans are and should be individualized. My philosophy is to keep the plan as simple and cost-efficient as possible, especially for the client who is doing preventative planning way in advance of any issues.

Have you found that you have needed to change your methods in recent years, because of FTC v. Affordable Media, or to include Nevis LLCs?

We do not believe that every client needs a foreign entity. Where there is a need, an offshore trust will be used and it is generally used in conjunction with a limited liability company. When such a plan is best for the client, we favor the Nevis LLC.

If you can, please briefly describe a "success" story, that is, an asset protection plan that was threatened in some way and withstood the attack, and why. Please change names as you think fit.

I can't pinpoint a specific success story as they have all been successful in my opinion. Sometimes the original plan has to be restructured as events unfold; however, none of my clients have had to neither relinquish all of their pro-

SUCCESS STORY: ARNOLD S. GOLDSTEIN

tected assets nor have they effectuated settlements that involved all of their funds. Therefore, they have all been successful.

In my forty-six years of practicing asset protection, I have not had any client's assets seized under one of the plans that I set up. Some of my clients have chosen to settle with their creditors, however, no client to date has been forced to unwind their plan and produce protected assets.

If you can, please briefly describe an unsuccessful story where assets were seized — this may well be the story of someone who came to you for advice after the lawsuit. Please change names as you think fit.

In my forty-six years as an asset protection attorney, no plan that I have created has ever been penetrated by a creditor.

If relevant, what changes did you recommend to improve the asset protection in this last case?

Each asset protection plan should be considered as an ongoing plan. Often, client's needs will change over time and therefore, I must restructure their plan with additions, adjustments, or deletions. My policy is to revisit my client's plan whenever they have a life changing event, add new assets, or they are feeling threatened by a potential creditor.

You may have heard a ton about foreign assets trusts, and it is true that some people favor them while others say that they are a waste of time. As always, the truth lies somewhere between the two extremes, and a chapter is devoted to discussing the pros and cons. Domestic trusts are also available in many forms and can be useful in certain circumstances.

And now, to approach a delicate subject: If you do not have a prenuptial agreement, you may be exposed to risks that you would like to avoid. This book includes, with suitable discretion, issues that are related to your more personal life, and how you can deal with them.

Finally, when you make your final exit, you will probably wish for your will to be done. Unfortunately, Uncle Sam often has a different idea, and unless you have made suitable arrangements, your loved ones may be left in an awfully different state from that which you intended. This is your final act of asset protection: to pass on to your heirs that which you have worked to achieve with minimum losses to the tax man.

There are many books and no shortage of advisers on asset protection, and it is my intention that you will be glad you picked up this one. In a thorough manner, all of your options are explained in a way that is easy to understand. There is no one solution that fits all with asset protection; it depends mostly on your personal situation and the form of your assets. Do not believe any gurus who advise you otherwise.

Sometimes, you will find seminars where the intention is to sell you on a particular solution, and I advise you to stay away, or at least not buy into their notion without being sure that it suits you. The law is still evolving and some techniques have not yet been fully tested in the courts. You should use this book as an authoritative source to educate yourself, and then make sure that your plans are implemented properly and legally with your own advisors. It is important to employ your own specialists to produce the necessary documents to make sure there has been no change in the protections discussed within this book.

CHAPTER

So You Do Not Need Asset Protection?

"Our constitution protects aliens, drunks, and U.S. Senators."
– Will Rogers

Y ou may think that you do not need asset protection. But, you have some idea in the back of your mind that maybe you should check it out, and that's why you have picked up this book. Even if you do not think that you have much exposure to lawsuits, some instinct is driving you to question that attitude.

Your instinct is sound – the same instinct that served you well when you started your own company, or landed that high-paying job by acing the interview is telling you to look into asset protection. But sadly many others in your position thought they did not need asset protection, and may have lost everything and had to start over again after the unexpected happened.

It is easy to think that you do not need asset protection — after all, what do you have that the guy down the road does not? Anyway, you do not do anything outrageous, you have not offended anyone that you know of, and you have insurance to cover the unforeseen difficulties of life.

If only life was that simple. The one chance in five that you will be sued next year becomes one chance in three if you are a doctor or business owner. If you have not been sued yet, then consider yourself lucky, and read this book quickly so that you can get on with detailed planning. It is amazing that asset protection is not higher on everyone's to-do list when you consider the statistics, but the fact is that many people only actually treat it seriously when they receive a legal notice, and by then, it may be too late to protect your assets.

THE ETHICAL BALANCE

Of course, there is always a discussion about the morality of squirreling your assets away so that your creditors cannot touch them, and with good reason. It is not ethical or moral to try to cheat someone out of what is rightfully theirs. It is not ethical to not pay your debts. Just look at what most people think about large businesses that trade and have their operations in the United States, but have head offices in some tax sanctuary so that they pay the least they can in taxes to the government.

But against that background, look at the number of what may be considered unjustified lawsuits that abound, in the hope that some may stick or be settled out of court for a decent reward. After all, who does not think that suing McDonalds because they serve hot coffee is a ridiculous exercise? But that case in 1994 had the potential for outrageous gains for the lady and the attorney involved, which were reduced on appeal from the $2.7 million to a total of less than $600,000.

In this case, there is no doubt that the coffee could, and did, cause severe injury to the buyer, but to brew coffee at a lower temperature would also cause complaints. Actually, a similar case brought in the United Kingdom was rejected, as the judge asserted that tea should be brewed with boiling water, and coffee brewed with nearly boiling water, so McDonalds had been acting properly in using water that hot. The argument of protecting us from ourselves has reached a higher legal level in the United States, and so you no longer have to just act reasonably, as the law used to aver, but also have to wrap anyone you come into contact with in cotton wool, just to be safe.

Most independent businesses fail within three years of their launch. A large amount of capital, time, energy, and personal sacrifice is needed to make an independent business succeed. Don't let this deter you, though, if you have a big, new idea for a product or service that you are sure consumers cannot live without—perhaps establishing an independent business is the way to go.

FRIVOLOUS LAWSUITS

Worse than that, there is also the class of truly frivolous lawsuits, which can strike at any time. By definition, the frivolous lawsuit has absolutely no basis in law — but they happen and can be costly to defend. If you are beginning to accumulate wealth, be assured that you may soon be on the radar of plaintiffs and attorneys that desire to secure their futures without earning them. Because of the cost of defending them, lawsuits are often settled out of court, which is a tactic that is indulged in and dependent upon some unscrupulous litigators.

It is not uncommon for a frivolous suit to make it to court, and once it has there may be no justification, but truth will not always succeed. Many lawyers work on the basis that the judge will allow a case to proceed, rationalizing that no matter how much speculation there is, everyone deserves the chance to have a hearing. Yet, many juries are inclined to believe that the case must have merit, on the basis that if it did not, the judge would not have allowed it to get to them. You can see this circular argument would work against you.

LAWSUIT POTENTIAL

If you have any doubts that this is a potentially serious problem, consider these facts about the United States:

- More than 15 million civil lawsuits are filed each year

- The total cost of tort cases is $200 billion each year

- Nearly one out of six jury awards is for more than $1 million

- More than 7 percent of U.S. companies have suffered a lawsuit costing over $5 million in the past five years.

You may be in business for yourself, and be quite aware of the dangers of the work you do and the possibility for lawsuits. On the other hand, you may think that you do not do anything that is risky. In either case, you remain a target if your assets are exposed. Certainly, if you have any rental property, as many people do once they start building wealth, you are incredibly exposed as you have little control over how the renters may harm themselves while you are at home. A tenant was shot dead in a back alley. The landlord was successfully sued for $27 million when it was held that the lighting was inadequate. There has not yet been a case of someone scalding themselves in the shower because the water was too hot bringing a lawsuit against the landlord, but that may just be a matter of time. The attitude of certain predatory attorneys, particularly those that advertise on television, should be a warning of the threats faced in our current society.

As further evidence that you are at risk, consider the springing up of Web sites that have a sole purpose that appears to encourage people to sue. It is true, the Internet has become a tool for those who would like to have lawsuits filed on their behalf with the possibility of large rewards. Such Web sites include **www.SueEasy.com**, **www.WhoCanISue.com**, and **www.LegalMatch.com**. These sites will put you in touch with an attorney for any particular grievance that they have listed. If this was not worrying enough, while you are waiting for your case to be decided you can get an advance on the settlement at **www.LawsuitFunding.com**.

Hopefully, the summary of the risks has convinced you that you need to look into the security of your assets without delay. But, you may be asking, 'how real is the threat anyway, no one has come after me as of yet?' To make it more real, perhaps you need to consider who might come after your property.

The big one, of course, is when someone files a lawsuit against you. Depending on the actual charges, this can be big enough to wipe you out. This is possibly why many cases are settled out of court — even though you may feel you may not have any liability. Just imagine that a jury may consider their place as one of Robin Hood, taking from the rich to give to the poor, add in how the plaintiff's attorney may characterize you as getting rich from exploiting others and being due for a fall, and you may just get scared enough about the possible consequences that you decide to buy your way out.

The lawsuit is likely to be about negligence, as this is the predominant type filed. Libel, slander, and battery are others, and most of them lead to a claim for money damages. Often the attorney is working on a contingency basis and gets about one-third of the damages for his effort. The attorney is looking for a settlement, as his income depends on not having to go through the whole court process every time, and often there will be some insurance coverage that he will be hoping to negotiate on.

CREDITORS

Aside from the threat of lawsuits, you may also face common creditors — secured and unsecured. Secured creditors include banks that hold mortgages. Ultimately they can foreclose on your property to reclaim their money. You cannot, of course, do anything to provide asset protection of your house from such a contract — the whole point of the secured loan is that the property is available as recompense. But, subsequent loans, such as a second mortgage on your house, are secondary to the first mortgage and lose their claim to the property if it is foreclosed. Of course, the debt does not go away so easily — you still owe the money — but they cannot claim your house to get paid back.

Unsecured creditors are not as lucky as the mortgage holder. They rely on your good name and honesty to get paid back, and so they may be out of luck in the short term. Again, just because they do not have property that they can seize to cover the debt, it does not mean that the debt goes away. They will have to sue you to be paid, and then try to enforce a judgment against any assets they can find. If the assets have a prior claim by a secured creditor, then they cannot be taken to satisfy the unsecured debt.

Who else may put a claim on your assets? Do not forget the commercial creditor. An example of this is when your bank lends you money. If you do not pay the creditor back, they will come after you with the force necessary to get their money. They normally do not care that it will cost more to recover the funds than they lent you in the first place. In most cases, though, not paying them back would fall under the immoral or unethical class of debts — you took the money which they lent you in good faith, and you are responsible for paying it back.

THE GOVERNMENT

There is a slightly different approach if you owe money to the government. If you owe money to the Internal Revenue Service (IRS), or to the state for taxes, then they did not loan you money in the first place. Although they will try their hardest to be paid, no one will lose their job if they do not manage to secure the funds.

The main ways that the IRS will try to get money is by levying your wages and by putting a lien on your real estate. If neither of these methods work, the IRS does not get paid. They are also the only creditor who has a limited amount of time in which to secure the payment — there is a statute of limitations on collecting tax debt.

On the other hand, other government departments have different powers and are much more likely to make your life a misery if you do not pay up. The Federal Trade Commission (FTC), for instance, which guards against fraud, is allowed to seize whatever assets it finds, and can order you to turn over any assets it cannot find. The FTC raids your business, taking away your computers, and freezes your bank accounts — all before you even go to trial.

But, the federal government has powers that can override state laws, due to the Supremacy Clause in the constitution. This means that they do not have to regard the state's homestead exemption as valid and can seize your home. That being said, the fact that federal laws overrule the state can be a benefit. It means you get protection for your retirement plan if it is governed by Employee

Retirement Income Security Act, a federal statute often referred to as ERISA, and state rules do not allow it to be touched.

When you think about asset protection, you also need to consider what the assets are that you are protecting. Some assets, such as your house or bank account, are obvious. There are different ways in which these can be secured from seizure. Others, however, are less tangible, and may include your business. You could ask yourself the question, "If I died tomorrow, what would happen to my business?" If the answer is that the business would fold, then it is unlikely that your creditors would want to seize it. But, if your business has valuable items such as inventory, vehicles, and computers, there would be a possibility that the creditor would try to seize them.

While, these are physical, actual objects, like your house, most businesses also have accounts receivable, which a creditor could attach money from these to satisfy the debt.

No doubt you are now reeling under the weight of all the assets you had not considered to be vulnerable, or even acknowledged that you have control over. Do not worry; within this book, you will find out about many different ways that your assets can be protected from your creditors. You work hard in your life building your reputation and trying to achieve financial security, and you need to ensure that you protect it adequately.

TAKING ACTION

To be sure, one approach is to do business in a fair and honest manner, taking special care to ensure that your clients are fully satisfied and that you never upset anyone you meet in the course of business. Many people, though, rely on this approach — it is estimated that nine out of ten Americans have only their liability insurance to protect them from the dramatic effects of a lawsuit. It is incredible to me that we can spend so much time building our businesses, negotiating carefully on contracts, seeking expert investment advice, and doing many other things to increase our net worth, and yet we never think to take steps to provide proper protection to our assets until we get hit by that first lawsuit.

Perhaps it is not so surprising. After all, only one in five adults have even written a simple will, and it is a certainty that every one of us will die one day. How less likely are we to deal with protection from lawsuits when we hardly expect to have one? The statistics show how wrong we are to take this view. There will be about 50 million lawsuits filed this year. There will be about five million deaths and injuries from car accidents. Would you even consider driving without car insurance? Then how can you consider not protecting yourself from a lawsuit?

Hopefully you are convinced of the need to take action along the lines of the recommendations in this book. The action you take must be considered. Take full account of your circumstances, as there are many possibilities for covering your assets and some are more suitable for particular situations than others. But you must take action, and this book will give you the knowledge and information that you need to know what you are talking about when you hire professional services to draw up the instruments of protection. Armed with your new knowledge, you will know exactly what the professionals are talking about, be able to deal with them efficiently without wasting their time, and be sure you are getting the best plan for your future protection.

CHAPTER 2

Plan Ahead

"Your life cannot go according to plan if you have no plan."
– Anonymous

Having decided that asset protection is an essential part of your portfolio, you now need to implement it. In this chapter, you will learn about the problems that arise if you wait until you need a plan to put one in place It is not that you cannot do anything to help protect yourself; it is that the law takes a dim view of someone who obviously wants to hide his assets from seizure once there is a valid claim on them.

The tax implications of securing your assets will also be discussed. It is appropriate that you consider the whole picture at once, as asset protection, by definition, has to take account of anything which impacts your assets, and tax is certainly one of those things. No doubt while you are reading, you will be able to determine a broad plan for structuring your assets which will be applicable to your particular needs, and I advise you to take notes to discuss with your professional advisers.

PROTECTION PLANNING

Planning for asset protection means planning to keep something of value safe. It involves taking steps to minimize the risk of creditors or other claimants being able to reach your assets. This can include setting up different business entities such as corporations or limited liability companies (LLC), and these will be explained later. Sometimes you will be able to protect several assets with one entity, and other times you may want to have different businesses for different assets. In each case, this book explains why the entity may be appropriate for you, along with the drawbacks of each.

It is important that you take the steps before you have any problems, or even a hint of a problem, from any creditor who may want to lay claim to your resources. The whole point of the recommended steps is that you should structure your life and assets to reduce your vulnerability. Then you are able to stand with impunity when someone threatens an outrageous lawsuit.

This cannot be stressed enough: the key to successful asset protection is to do it before you need it. There can be legal consequences to creating asset protection mechanisms after your business has been attacked. Many judges will dismiss legal tactics taken to protect your assets after you have already been slapped with lawsuits by creditors or others seeking to take your assets. Planning is the first and almost certainly the most critical of all steps in the asset protection process.

An incomplete plan can create more problems for you than it solves. You must identify all your assets and understand which assets have automatic legal, state, and federal protection in full or in part from seizure, and which ones you need to take action to protect by means of your asset protection plan. The federal and state automatic protections are used every day to save necessary assets in the case of bankruptcy, and you need to know what they are to identify your areas of vulnerability for the rest. A critical component of this is understanding how the ownership structure of business assets will affect your future ability to protect those assets, knowing the ownership structures on which you can rely, and which you can maximize under the legal allowance.

Even though there is no such thing as a perfect asset protection plan, the idea is to establish plausible goal, creating a plan as close to perfection as you can, and to understand and include all the critical assets of your business so you will avoid problems in the future. There are guidelines available, which will be covered in this book, to help you create a plan.

DUAL THREATS

Let's also be clear from the start — there are two basic viewpoints you have to deal with, and unless you take care of them both, you will remain dramatically exposed. You must plan to take care of both areas of threat so that you can sleep well at night. These two areas are your personal life and your business.

Consider that you, your spouse, or your teenage son or daughter could quite possibly have an unfortunate accident in your car. In this accident, the extent of the injury to other passengers in the car left you exposed beyond the limits of your insurance. This is a liability on your personal life and assets, and you want to be adequately protected from losing everything. But what if the plaintiff's attorney found out, as he would, that you owned a business? You need to have a protection plan in place that prevents your business from being decimated by a personal claim against you or members of your family.

From the other side, if there was an accident at your business, or someone slipped and fell in the parking lot at work, how would you cope with that? The business could get sued, and indeed some would say it should be if there was any negligence involved. Your insurance may cover it all, or there may be an exception to the type of loss, or it might exceed your limits. But what about your home, personal assets, and bank account? If you do not have a suitable asset protection plan in place for your business, the attorney might come after your personal assets to make up any shortfall, and could even drive you into bankruptcy. If you employ people, you are exposed to lawsuits from your employees, whether justified or not, and also from the public. Both sides of the situation must be addressed.

Your plan should be concerned with the diversification of ownership of your assets. This is an issue that will focus on both the optional ownership structure of your assets and the ownership forms you should avoid. The idea of protecting your assets is linked to protection from inside threats and also those coming from outside the business.

For example, let's say you are a doctor in private practice and one of your nurses misreads your instructions and gives the wrong dosage of medicine to a patient. The patient may sue you and the nurse for malpractice, taking all that you have worked for with them. While it is not necessarily your fault, you are the one who has the deep pockets and quite possibly insurance, so you will be involved in the suit.

Another instance may be where you are a successful building contractor hiring out hundreds of workers for projects. One of those workers falls from a beam and dies, leaving you with a hefty wrongful death suit from his family. While insurance may cover some of your losses in both instances, it can never make up for the large amount a judge may order you to pay.

MAKING IT DIFFICULT

One of the tricks to asset protection is to make the task of the creditor, who is trying to take your assets, difficult. If his attorney sees that you have taken time to structure your affairs so that it is costly and difficult to pay dividends and reach your assets, then it is likely that he will advise his client not to bother, deciding that it would not be worth his time on a contingency fee basis. This will discourage the filing of frivolous lawsuits and may save you some heartache.

It is not always possible to completely shield all your assets, and, as the law is being developed all the time, no one can guarantee infallibility. The reality may be that nothing can ever be exempt from anything. According to John Porter, former professor of media studies at Washington University in St. Louis, anyone can sue anyone for anything.

"The trick is to locate all different kinds of corporate hurdles to cross to make it harder for anyone to sue you," Porter explains. "Laws apply that can pierce the corporate veil."

From the earliest of times of the caveman, who tried to protect his food, shelter, clothing, and tools from marauders; to land owners of the middle ages, who would entrust their property to the Church to prevent seizure by the government; to modern-day practices of sheltering financially valuable assets to prevent them from being taken by creditors' lawsuits, humans have practiced asset protection in one form or another. The experts say that while there are statutes that apply, to one degree or another, to the protection of one's essential assets such as future retirement income, homes, or insurance policies, there actually is no "body of law" that protects the assets of an individual. It is up to every individual, with the wise counsel of financial and investment planning experts, to determine legitimate ways to protect against a risk of legal action.

Let's be clear, though — we are not talking about shady schemes to wriggle out of paying legitimate debts. It is using asset protection for such things that can give it somewhat of a dodgy reputation, and I would never condone planning to cheat creditors for your own greed. Asset protection is about protecting your life savings from seizure; preventing your business from being disabled from operation; stopping the suspension of trading while you have to deal with unfounded claims. While we could most likely discuss all day what constitutes fair and unfair seizure, and we might have different views on what was justified, there is no doubt that you need to have the security of the amount of protection that the law allows you to have. If you truly are culpable and think that some recompense is due to the claimant, effective asset protection means that you can negotiate out of court from a position of strength and give only truly fair compensation.

Much of the work of asset protection, after the initial strategic planning and the proper steps have been taken, occurs in the courtroom. New strategies for assets protection are being created periodically as old ones become too popular and are hit by various legal rulings and courtroom strategies. As cases are taken to court and rulings are set down, they become case law for creditors and others to follow in an effort to succeed in their legal actions. True asset protection planners stay aware of strategies, tactics, and court cases to be able to creatively come up with viable, new approaches that have not yet been tested in court. Strategies can be built up from both the court tested techniques and new creative approaches to get the optimum protection; and the best strategies work to keep you out of the courtroom.

While you may be able to anticipate likely sources of lawsuits, it is not my intention that you only shield yourself against them. To the extent that you are able to, you need to protect yourself from unanticipated problems, by definition things that cannot be foreseen, and a full asset protection program will do this. The fact is that lawsuits can come from anywhere and anyone.

ASSETS OWNERSHIP

In structuring the best plan for your situation, a key consideration is the ownership of different types of assets. Some of these should certainly be kept separate from one another to create the greatest level of protection, even if this means that you have to set up several business organizations. If you are considering using foreign or offshore trusts, you should carefully consider the country that you are setting up the trust in because it will be subject to the laws of that particular country. There may be a threat to your assets that only arises because you are setting up a corporate entity or trust in a particular country or state, and you must ensure that you have expert advice from someone knowledgeable in the laws of that place. Otherwise you may find that you have caused yourself a greater problem as a result of trying to address the original issue.

As part of your planning procedure, you will need to consider three areas: the creation of an asset diversification plan, a liability analysis, and a summary of any additional protection you will need in the case of a business failure.

Diversification is not just concerned about the broad ownership structure of your assets, but is also concerned with isolating each ownership structure from the other. This means that different asset types can be kept separate from each other and achieve optimal diversification.

In your liability analysis, you need to identify and understand your potential liabilities, and also consider the possible legal consequences of those liabilities. This is critical in creating a viable asset protection plan. You need to identify what areas are particularly vulnerable, as this can help you avoid disaster before it happens.

INSURANCE

Finally, despite it not being the all-protecting element that people think it is, insurance is important in completing your asset protection plan. What you have to do is use it as a component in your plan and not think that you can depend on it to substitute for planning — otherwise you may find that you are in difficulties and have no fallback. Liability and property insurance can provide protection against loss of assets following a courtroom judgment. With any luck, the asset planning strategies will have been able to prevent any attempt by a plaintiff to get past your defenses.

Insurance can be the last line of defense against devastating loss. Just as you insure your automobile in case you experience a loss due to theft, damage, or liability suits, you can create a portfolio of insurance products to cover your various assets and keep them as safe as possible. Liability insurance protects your assets against damage levied against you if another person is injured or another's property is harmed by something you do. Property insurance is designed to protect your own property, like your car, home, or business structure, from damage to it that is caused by another person or "acts of God," such as a fire, flood, or tornado.

No one wants to file an insurance claim because the automatic result will be that your insurance premiums go up. But the potential financial devastation of a legal judgment against you or your business is far more frightening than a potential increase in your premiums. Plus, the goal will be to structure your asset protection plan to prevent the need to rely on liability insurance to pay off a personal or professional claim against you.

The following is a case study of Mark Nestmann, who has experience dealing with wealth preservation, international tax planning and off-shore investments.

CASE STUDY: MARK NESTMANN

In what way are you involved with asset protection, and does this include general estate planning and tax issues?

Asset protection is often the central issue in which our clients are concerned. However, asset protection is controversial and for that reason we endeavor to set up for our clients an integrated estate plan, both domestic and international, with the incidental effect of providing asset protection. Domestic and international tax planning is an integral part of this process.

Do you specialize in any particular aspects of asset protection, such as foreign trusts or LLCs?

We don't have an asset protection specialty, again, to avoid calling attention to the asset protection aspects of the plan. For instance, with a foreign LLC, we would counsel the client that there are numerous non-asset-protection uses for such an entity, such as more convenient access to non-U.S. investments, and the ability to gift interests of the LLC to family members and potentially achieve valuation discounts for estate planning purposes. We do not generally recommend single-member LLCs, domestic or foreign, if asset protection is a concern of the client. This is due to a series of U.S. court decisions making it clear that charging order protection may not exist for single-member LLCs.

In your experience, do you find that a single entity or strategy is sufficient for most people, or do you commonly recommend a multi-layered structure?

Our experience is all over the map here. Some low-risk clients may not need any entity at all, particularly if they live in a state with strong homestead pro-

CASE STUDY: MARK NESTMANN

tections and the bulk of their assets is in their home or in retirement plans protected by state or federal law. High-risk clients may require an offshore private annuity, or offshore trust, tied to one or more offshore companies or LLCs. The decision on which entity or entities to use, if any, is entirely driven by the client's facts and circumstances.

Have you found that you have needed to change your methods in recent years, because of FTC v. Affordable Media, or to include Nevis LLCs?

Yes, absolutely. We have de-emphasized the use of offshore trusts, particularly in standalone structures. In addition, we now use private annuities funded with after-tax dollars much more frequently as a planning alternative to offshore trusts.

Describe a success story where an asset protection plan was threatened in some way and withstood the attack, and why that happened. Please change names as you think fit.

We have been fortunate enough to not have any of our plans attacked directly. However, there have been a few threatened attacks. In every case the client was able to settle the claim within either the limits of existing liability insurance or by making a token payment to the person or entity threatening the client. We believe this was possible due to the attacker realizing that the cost of attacking the plan would far exceed that of litigating against the client.

Briefly describe an unsuccessful story where assets were seized — this may well be the story of someone who came to you for advice after the lawsuit. Please change names as you think fit.

Fortunately, we have not experienced any situations where a client's assets were seized after we constructed a plan. However, in one situation, an individual contacted us after they had experienced a judgment in a personal

CASE STUDY: MARK NESTMANN

injury case. Unfortunately, due to the facts of the case we weren't able to assist this individual and eventually, the individual experienced an asset seizure.

If relevant, what changes did you recommend to improve the asset protection in this last case?

This individual would have been well served to increase limits of his liability coverage and to construct an integrated asset protection plan well in advance of any litigation.

Mark Nestmann is a journalist and public speaker with more than 20 years of investigative experience and the author of many books and reports dealing with wealth preservation, international tax planning, and offshore investing. His consulting firm, The Nestmann Group, Ltd., provides wealth preservation and international tax planning services. Nestmann is an Associate Member of the American Bar Association (member of subcommittee on Foreign Activities of U.S. Taxpayers, Committee on Taxation) and member of the Society of Professional Journalists. In 2005, he was awarded a Masters of Law (LLM) degree in international tax law at the Vienna (Austria) University of Economics and Business Administration. Nestmann also serves as a contributing editor to The Sovereign Society (www.sovereignsociety.com).

Mark Nestmann, President, The Nestmann Group, Ltd
2303 N. 44th St. #14-1025 • Phoenix, AZ 85008 USA.
Tel. / Fax (USA): +1 (602) 604-1524
E-mail: info@nestmann.com • Web: www.nestmann.com

ASSETS LIST

Ownership is a foundation of asset protection. What you do not own or apparently have no control over is clearly protected from seizure by your tormentors. In the simplest terms, how can you be expected to hand over that which you do not own and cannot get? As you read through this book, you will see various ways in which ownership can be assigned to companies or other entities, which will render your possessions relatively inaccessible to your creditors.

One of the preliminary stages of setting up an asset protection plan is to determine what assets you have. You may be surprised when you start thinking to find how many different things you have in your name. Of course, some of the things are obvious, such as your house and your bank account. I advise you to list them out and check who is the legal owner of each asset — sometimes you will find that, for instance, real estate is not actually titled in the way you think it is. There is a table in the Appendix for your use.

Your assets list will include:

- Personal residence

- Real estate property — land and buildings and other non-liquid assets

- Vehicles

- Retirement and benefits — pensions, Individual Retirement Accounts (IRAs), simplified employee pension plans

- Tools of the trade, inventory

- Personal property

- Life insurance cash value/face value

- Furniture and office furnishing

- Current assets — accounts and notes receivable

- Brokerage accounts, bank accounts, and CDs

- Disability income and insurance coverage

- Long-term care insurance

- Ownership interests, limited partnerships, unrealized investments

- Commodities such as gold or other precious metals that you own

Please do not assume that this list is exhaustive, as I do not know you, your life, and activities. Though, it should give you a good start to making up your own list.

You should detail separately the assets that you own as an individual, the assets that you own with your spouse, and those that are owned by your business. This is a good first step in asset protection planning. If you work from home, your computer, your office equipment, and perhaps even your car, if you use it to go to appointments, could be items that you want to consider the ownership of carefully. Of course, your car is a special case, as you no doubt use it for personal matters as well. You need to be careful in the ownership and in deciding who or what should take title of your possessions so that you can maximize your protection – while bearing in mind that you do not know if the threat will materialize from your business operation or from your private life.

Although this book is about asset protection, there are other aspects that you may want to include in any plan that you make. Once you have defined your assets and have some idea of the hazards that may threaten them, including your business operations, you should consider carefully what you want for your goals and achievements. What other items do you want to bear in mind when you put together your plan? Do you have a family business that you have built from scratch and wish to pass on to your offspring? Or do you have family heirlooms and antiques, or maybe even a family home, which you would prefer to be handed on intact to your heirs? You want to make sure it is as difficult as possible for anyone to go after these things in settlement of a claim against you or against your business.

On the other hand, you may have partners or colleagues in a professional business, which is likely to attract lawsuits, and your concern is to lock up the business equity to the extent possible so that the practice can continue — this is typical of health practitioners. Perhaps you need to sit down with your partners, and run through the options calmly and thoroughly. If you do not define clear goals, you may find that your planning does not produce all the results that you want, and it is no time to discover the errors when they are revealed to you by a lawsuit.

In summary, your asset protection planning must be carefully considered, but should be implemented as soon as possible, in conjunction with professional advisers who can prepare the documentation. In truth, it should be part of a larger financial plan that covers all aspects of your finances. There are impacts on income, corporate, estate, and gift taxes. There are even, as you will see, possible impacts should you and your spouse decide to separate. What you prepare now will affect your retirement, perhaps significantly, depending on how well you plan. Set yourself a reading goal, and digest the information that follows so that you will not remain one of the countless people who did not know it could happen to them. This way, you can sleep more easily at night.

CHAPTER

3

No Escaping

"To predict the behavior of ordinary people in advance, you only have to assume that they will always try to escape a disagreeable situation with the smallest possible expenditure of intelligence."
– Friedrich Nietzsche

For Nietzsche's commentary on the human condition to be complete, we should add the phrase "and the smallest possible expenditure of effort." This typifies the attitude that most people have — we wait until disaster strikes before taking any steps to avoid the consequences of that disaster in the first place. Unfortunately for those who subscribe to this view, while there may be some areas of human endeavor where this is sufficient, asset protection is not one of them.

FRAUDULENT TRANSFERS

The point of this chapter is to say, and to emphasize, that "fraudulent transfers" or "fraudulent conveyances" are what you do when you do not plan ahead, and they may not be upheld. Fraudulent transfers are defined as asset transfers made to hinder, delay, or defraud creditors; transfers that are for less than the real value, or "reasonably equivalent value" when you are leaving yourself short of cash; and transfers made while you are insolvent to pay "insiders." This is the reason that the last chapter emphasized taking action now, before you have a problem. Because it is important that you understand this concept and the dangers of depending on a potentially fraudulent transfer, the many forms they can take and the remedies creditors can seek are detailed in this book.

Fraud is defined in the Uniform Fraudulent Transfer Act (UFTA), which is used by many states. It is also defined in the Uniform Fraudulent Conveyance Act (UFCA) which is used by some other states. The provisions of the acts are incredibly similar. They are both designed to stop the obvious trick of trying to divest yourself of your assets to a cooperative party when you are being sued or when you think that you are going to be sued. If these laws were not in place, then plaintiffs everywhere would be cheated out of their compensation by anyone with no asset protection plan but half a clue.

ACTUAL FRAUD

Fraudulent transfers can be separated into two types. The first we will look at is actual fraud, sometimes called fraud in fact. For actual fraud to have taken place, the creditor has to show that the transfer was made with intent to hinder, delay, or defraud him. The law requires that the creditor show intent, in other words that you meant to disadvantage his restitution in some way. As this depends on your state of mind, this can be difficult to demonstrate.

Over the years, the courts have tackled this problem by putting together badges of fraud — acts that provide a strong indication that you meant to defraud the creditor. The badges of fraud are spelled out in the UFTA, and can be broken down to the following:

- Were the assets transferred to an insider, such as a close family member or friend?

- Did you continue to use the assets after transfer — was the giving just a sham?

- Did you try to hide the transfer — this implies that you had something to hide?

- Did you receive less than market value in return for the assets? People do not frequently give away assets without receiving something in return, unless they want to defraud their creditors.

- Was the transfer made after you had been sued or threatened with a lawsuit?

- Did you make yourself insolvent, that is, make your assets less than your liabilities, by transferring the asset?

Just because the transfer satisfies one or more of the badges of fraud does not automatically mean that it constitutes actual fraud — it just provides some evidence to help in that assessment. The court will look at whether the transfer is something that would occur in the normal course of business, or whether it is trying to take away assets to avoid their seizure. And some transfers may be made that show up under the badge of fraud, but are perfectly justified. For instance, it would be quite in order for you to make your regular mortgage payment, even if that left you short of cash for the creditor. It is obvious that it is normal and expected that you make the payment.

CONSTRUCTIVE FRAUD

With the problem of showing intent, it is hard for creditors to demonstrate actual fraud. This brings me to the second type of fraudulent transfer, which is called constructive fraud. This is totally different, as your transfer can be fraudulent even when you act innocently and without intent to defraud your creditors. Considering the problem of proving intent, discussed above, constructive fraud is at least a provable act, and thus a more practical measure for the courts of justice.

Constructive fraud exists when you give away or sell property for less than its fair value; and you are insolvent at the time or the gift makes you insolvent. Both conditions must be satisfied to prove constructive fraud.

The first condition can be fairly obvious if it is a gift, but if you receive a benefit for the assets, then the whole question of fair value enters into the equation, and that is something that can require some discretion in interpretation. The fair value is commonly defined as how much a prudent seller would get when selling the assets in a reasonable way. This does not mean though that it is what you may usually consider to be fair market value.

This depends sometimes on what type of asset is being disposed of. For instance, if you sell publicly traded shares for less than they are quoted on the stock exchange, it is reasonable to say that you did not get fair value. On the other hand, if they are shares in a private company, or if they are antiques or collectible items, there is room for dispute. Actually, some courts have held that real estate sold for 70 percent of its appraised value still satisfies the fair value test; that is, the sale was not constructive fraud.

It is interesting to note that any time you sell something for less than its fair value, there is a possibility that a claim may come up concerned with some previous action that can find this as being constructive fraud. This is because there is no question of intent in the constructive fraud criteria. Say you have a building company and some of your previous work is defective — perhaps one of your workers left out necessary reinforcement. The fact that you do not know this does not come into it. When it is discovered by a massive collapse, any assets that you have disposed of for less than fair value since the time of the construction can be examined for constructive fraud.

The other condition that has to be determined for constructive fraud to be established is the one of insolvency. Essentially, this measures whether you have enough assets to meet your liabilities or pay your bills when they come due. Put simply, you are not permitted by the fraud law to get rid of your assets at less than the fair value if the result is that you have no money left for your creditor. It does not matter if you did not have enough money for your creditors before the sale, or if the sale puts you in that situation. In either case, to cheaply sell off your assets would be evidence of fraud. It is easy to see why such an action in the face of the debt would be construed as fraud, as it would be cheating your creditor from possible recompense.

There is no doubt that fraudulent transfer laws are incredibly complex in application and subject to interpretation by the courts. Despite being seemingly simple in definition, they are actually mostly in a gray area, not clearly fraudulent but also not completely non-fraudulent. If you get stuck in this situation, you need to be sure you have experienced professionals advising you to get the best opinions.

CONSEQUENCES

You may be wondering what happens if you are found guilty of a fraudulent transfer. As noted above, the result may simply be an "unwinding" of the transfer to make it as if it had never happened — this might explain why some people think they can still try to get away with transferring their assets once they are threatened with a lawsuit. Yet, it is much more secure to protect your assets before this happens.

The courts only try to restore the situation to what it was before the fraudulent transfer. Arthur S. Goldstein points out in his book *So Sue ME!* that fraudulent transfer in itself is not a crime, but a civil remedy to reverse the transaction. A recent Supreme Court judgment in Florida states that "a fraudulent conveyance action is not an action against a debtor for failure to pay an amount owing from a prior judgment and does not warrant an additional judgment against the same debtor because of the fraudulent conveyance." The lawsuit is not against the debtor, but against the property or the person holding the property. Certainly if you found yourself unprepared, you could still attempt to put your assets out of reach of your potential creditor, though this would not be considered a worthwhile course of action by some attorneys. Only after the creditor has won a judgment can he start to progress a fraudulent transfer claim; there is no restriction preventing transfer before the case is decided.

The remedies that the court may award to the creditor are, first and foremost, calling the transfer invalid and restoring the title to the assets so that it may be part of the settlement. Additionally, it can freeze the assets to prevent further transfers that may be attempted to put it out of reach again. Actually, the court can even appoint a receiver to take charge over the assets if they are considered likely to disappear. The court can decide to award damages, particularly to cover the costs incurred by the creditor in recovering the assets, and the court can also recover any proceeds received from the transfer. Note that this does not apply if the assets have been sold subsequently to a purchaser paying a fair value.

Having said that, the law does not require that you do not dispose of your assets pending a judgment, even though many people believe this. The fact is, until the judgment has happened, the creditor has no recognizable legal claim to any of your assets, so they cannot be constrained.

Because there are clearly defined rules about constructive fraud, you might think you have little chance of escaping the judgment if that is what you have done. What the courts tend to do, though, is a sort of "smell test," to see whether they believe the transfer to be fraudulent. If there is another valid reason for the transfer other than hindering or delaying the creditor getting the asset, then you may be able to defeat the claim. Barbara Black has had considerable success with frustrating creditor seizure of assets even after a lawsuit has been filed.

CASE STUDY: BARBARA BLACK

Barbara Black has had a long and successful career, with 20 years of consulting exclusively about asset protection. She attained a MA in Finance from the University of Missouri in 1980, and an MBA from the University of Arizona, Entrepreneurship Program 1987.

Barbara Black can be contacted toll free at 1-866-287-2289.

E-mail: bblack@bulletproofasset.com • Web site: **www.bulletproofasset.com**

In what way are you involved with asset protection, and does this include general estate planning and tax issues?

Our primary focus is protecting clients from lawsuits and creditors. All the structures and strategies we use are to achieve that result. We do some estate planning via living trusts, pour-over wills, and U.S. Grantor trusts. We are not CPAs, but advise clients of reduction in estate taxes that comes from using certain structures such as a family limited partnership with a living trust.

Do you specialize in any particular aspects of asset protection, such as foreign trusts or LLCs?

We specialize in U.S. Grantor trusts registered in Belize or the Cook Islands, asset-protected NV family limited partnerships, and asset-protected NV LLCs. We also do international business corporations and international LLCs in selective jurisdictions, but offshore corporations are only a very small part of our business.

CASE STUDY: BARBARA BLACK

In your experience, do you find that a single entity or strategy is sufficient for most people, or do you commonly recommend a multi-layered structure?

Rarely is a single entity sufficient for most people. A multi-layered structure is extremely important in asset protection for many reasons – primarily separating out 'safer' family assets from 'riskier' investment assets such as rental property or business equipment/inventory/accounts receivable. In our experience, layering is essential in discouraging predatory attacks as it makes the client too 'hard' to attack and causes them to be abandoned in favor of someone 'easier' to attach judgments liens or charging orders to. Multi-layering is essential in implementing a collapsing bridge strategy for severe attacks.

Have you found that you have needed to change your methods in recent years, because of FTC v. Affordable Media, or to include Nevis LLCs?

We have formed Nevis LLCs upon request for many years. In our experience, using only an offshore corporation is not an effective form of asset protection for clients who lose lawsuits. This is because ownership of an offshore corporation cannot be hidden, and a judge can legally compel a client to return the assets to the U.S. to pay the judgment, or face contempt of court charges and jail time until they do voluntarily return the assets.

When adding an offshore component to our clients' asset protection, we do an international asset protection trust formed in such a way that the client cannot legally be compelled to return assets, nor can the foreign trustee be compelled to do so and no attorney or judge in the U.S. can successfully pursue control of those assets from the foreign jurisdiction.

Asset protection methods have changed over the past few years but primarily in the offshore arena. Effective domestic asset protection has not changed as much. The operating agreement is the heart of the protection for domestic asset protection entities and that is a fluid document that can be changed as needed to meet the times.

CASE STUDY: BARBARA BLACK

Briefly describe a success story, that is, an asset protection plan that was threatened in some way and withstood the attack, and why. Please change names as you think fit.

Jill and Bob Anderson came to us this year already with a lawsuit by medical creditors for $150,000 for unpaid medical bills. The creditors had refused to work with them.

Trying to protect assets after a lawsuit has been filed and especially when the lawsuit is brought by creditors is an area many asset protection firms will not even touch, due to fraudulent conveyance laws.

Our solution was first to form a NV family limited partnership to equity strip their home, and hold their rental properties and accounts. A passive NV LLC that they owned and controlled was formed to serve as general partner of the partnership.

In addition we had the clients work directly with our offshore trust company to form and register an international asset protection trust for the purpose of investing in real estate in Belize and the Cook Islands. The clients were instructed to actively research properties there, work with a local realtor and keep a record of all calls and paperwork including brochures and price quotes sent to them by the realtor.

Once formed, they asked their U.S. trustee to resign, thereby throwing control of the trust (and of the partnership) to the offshore trust company in Belize. Belize has no statutes on fraudulent conveyance and does not honor any other country's statutes on fraudulent conveyance. Because the trust was formed directly with them and not via a U.S. asset protection firm and because it was formed for a business reason to invest in real estate, their medical creditors who won the lawsuit were unsuccessful in either attaching any of their assets or convincing a judge of charging them with fraudulent conveyance.

CASE STUDY: BARBARA BLACK

Briefly describe an unsuccessful story where assets were seized — this may well be the story of someone who came to you for advice after the lawsuit. Please change names as you think fit.

The majority of our clients come to us after they have already been served with a lawsuit or are behind in credit payments. We have not had a single client lose assets yet, so long as they are willing to spend the money required and follow our instructions. It costs considerably more for a client to protect themselves after the fact than it does to set up pro-active protection before any lawsuit or creditor attack occurs. We have developed a three-tiered system that puts assets out of reach of creditors and lawsuits while avoiding charges of fraudulent conveyance and making it legally impossible for a client to be compelled to undo a structure or bring assets back into the judge's jurisdiction for seizure.

The few clients who have lost assets have, in every case, refused to do everything we recommended they do, either doing it only partially or not at all, largely because of cost, resulting in being compelled by a judge to undo what they had done. These were clients who formed only an international business corporation, or clients who formed a domestic entity very late in their lawsuit or creditor attack, and refused to add an international asset protection trust to own that entity to collapse control of their assets offshore. If you only form a domestic entity late in the game, a judge can deem the timing to be fraudulent conveyance and compel you to undo the structure to allow the assets to be seized.

If relevant, what changes did you recommend to improve the asset protection in this last case?

An international asset protection trust properly formed is essential for putting assets out of reach from aggressive attack and for making it impossible for the client to undo the structure. In some cases, if formed late in the lawsuit or attack, the client must set up the trust directly with our foreign trust company and for a specific business purpose to avoid fraudulent conveyance charges. They must then follow up and perform the actions necessary to fulfill that business purpose for the trust. Then, the fact that the trust also protects the assets held in the domestic structure is incidental.

NOT FRAUDULENT

As an interesting note: it can never be a fraudulent transfer if you prefer one creditor over another. If you did not want to pay a particular creditor and owe other creditors, you can pay them, even if this does not leave you enough money for the original creditor. You can select whom you favor with being paid back. You can even extend this idea and pay more than you have to towards another debt, to shield your money. This would apply, for example, if you prepaid some, or all, of your mortgage. This would not be considered a fraudulent transfer because you are paying a genuine creditor, even though you did not have to pay them so much so soon.

Another situation in which the transfer is not fraudulent is when you dispose of an asset and receive fair value for it. It is never a fraudulent transfer to receive fair value for an asset because one of the aspects of proving the fraud is to show that you received inadequate compensation for the assets. The disposal has not diminished your total worth, and therefore has not harmed your creditor's position.

Where this can get into fascinating legal territory is if you do not actually receive cash, but instead, a promissory note. This could be secured on the property by a deed of trust, and the note could require that interest be paid at the market rate. Now, the transfer is not fraudulent as the interest rate is not unusual, but the creditor and his attorney will have to wait and receive each interest payment as it becomes due, a little each year, until the amount commanded by the court has been received. This incremental payment over time can be a strong incentive to the creditor and his attorney to accept a lower lump sum payment in settlement.

While this is a possible cause of action, the safest way to proceed is to protect your assets before you see any sign of a problem. That way, you can choose the most advantageous arrangements, which can take into account tax and inheritance matters, and you can feel fairly confident that the transfer of title in the property will not be challenged later. Certainly, you will find that the choices you have are diminished and possibly less desirable if you wait to be sued before making these arrangements.

CHAPTER 4

I Thought I Was Exempt?

"In human life there is constant change of fortune; and it is unreasonable to expect an exemption from the common fate. Life itself decays, and all things are daily changing."
– Plutarch

When Plutarch, a first century Greek thinker, wrote those words, he was concerned with avoiding the common fate. Some people in modern America believe that there are exemptions that will spare them from their financial fate if sued, but, unfortunately for them, there is an immense variation throughout the states and with the Federal laws, so reliance on exemptions is at best a difficult topic, and certainly one which requires professional help for your particular circumstance.

To start with one famous example of exemptions, consider O.J. Simpson. He still owes $32 million. He has a house in Miami. He collects a six-figure annual pension. His insurance cannot be touched under Florida law. His wages cannot be garnished. Some of these protections arise from Federal law, but many are related to the state laws of Florida, where he resides, and its exemptions.

Most people are not able to organize their lives to this extent, and if you do not live in Florida, you may find significantly less protection under law. The case of O.J. Simpson is exceptional, but a clear demonstration of the power of exemption laws. When you are considering the assets that you wish to protect, a good starting point is determining which assets are, or could be made, exempt under law, and also determining the scope or amount that would be covered.

To start, the idea of legal exemptions is that they protect, for instance, a family whose wage earner is being threatened with asset seizure. The law will have some coverage for an individual person, but may also increase the exemptions where dependents are involved. Also, there is some protection for essentials, such as the homestead protection and shielding of retirement funds. These vary wildly between different states, so this chapter will acquaint you with the various types of shelter that you may find so that you may be an informed client for a specialist in your locality to confirm the details.

RETIREMENT EXEMPTIONS

Thinking first about retirement plans, you may be pleased to hear that every ERISA-qualified plan is lawsuit proof — at least fairly proof. This is how O.J. Simpson has managed to keep his NFL pension. That is because it is covered by federal laws, which override other rules. An ERISA-qualified plan can still yield to the IRS, sometimes to a spouse, and is also vulnerable if you do not have at least one non-owner enrolled in the plan.

Retirement plans may be 401(k) plans, pension plans (defined benefit plans), and profit sharing plans (defined contribution plans), and universal wisdom is to contribute as much as possible to them, as they are tax advantaged and often there is an element of employer matching contribution. Of course, with most Americans saving far too little for retirement, the universal wisdom is ignored by many, especially while Americans implicitly relying on a Social Security system that is increasingly rumored to be in financial difficulty. As you are taking the time and care to organize your affairs for asset protection, you may be a part of the minority who contributes effectively.

All of these plans can be covered by the ERISA of 1974. A key requirement of the Act is the pension plan prohibits gifting or assigning the assets. The IRS has to review the plan to make sure it complies, for its own tax relief purposes, and if it approves the plan, granting the tax relief, it is called a qualified plan. In simple terms, because you are normally unable to access the funds for your own use, they are also commonly inaccessible for creditors. How can you hand over something over which you do not have control?

One key factor for a qualifying plan is nondiscrimination — that is, you cannot expect a plan that is just for your executives to comply and be accepted as a qualified plan. Broadly speaking, though, it is not difficult to write a plan that will be approved; the language used is boilerplate. A qualifying plan has two parts — the plan itself and the trust. An outside trustee may administer the trust; the employees are called the beneficiaries.

Prior to 1992, there was some confusion whether an ERISA-qualified plan was always creditor-protected. In that year, the rules were tested in the Supreme Court, and, as so often happens, the decision clarified the intent and provided case law that can be relied on by reference to the ruling. The result of the decision is that an ERISA-qualified plan cannot be claimed to satisfy a creditor, even through a bankruptcy. You can make extra contributions, if allowed by your plans rules, to an ERISA-qualified plan in the face of a creditor's claim, and even if your remaining non-plan assets leave you insolvent, it cannot be reversed as a fraudulent transfer — a federal statute will always beat a state law.

The exceptions to the protection offered include the IRS and possibly spouses. An ERISA-qualified plan is covered by the Supremacy Clause, and is exempt from seizure by anyone other than Federal agencies or spouses. It cannot even be seized by a state in settlement of state tax debt. The Supremacy Clause does not apply to a federal agency, so the IRS has access to these funds.

As far as spouses go, there is a provision in the Act that permits a divorce judge to issue a Qualified Domestic Relations Order (QDRO). If this is issued and served on the plan administrator, he must comply with it. The Order cannot give the spouse any more rights than the employee has. It is interesting to note that a creditor of your spouse cannot get access to your assets in the ERISA-qualified plan, though, even in a community property state, where in theory everything is jointly owned.

Keep in mind that not all retirement plans qualify under this legislation. The breakdown between plans that have asset protection and those that do not is commonly along the lines of employer-sponsored plans, which come under ERISA, and employee-maintained plans, which do not and are thus vulnerable.

Employee-directed plans include IRAs and SEPs. These do not come under ERISA, and thus are open to creditors in some cases. Keogh Plans with multiple participants enjoy the same protections as ERISA-qualified plans, and are therefore commonly safe from creditors.

Many people have IRAs, and you may have even rolled over an ERISA plan into one when you left employment. It is common to roll the proceeds from a 401(k) into a personal IRA; it is a good idea for tax reasons, but terrible for asset protection. ERISA offers no protection for an IRA. If you have an ERISA-qualified plan that will accept the funds, it is possible to reverse the process and put your IRA funds into a secure account before they are threatened.

But before you rush into doing this, you should check on the status of your IRA where you live. The position at the time of writing is summarized in the Appendix. You see, many states have laws that fully protect non-qualified retirement accounts. A few states have no protection, but most have some sort of coverage, perhaps based on an amount that they calculate will provide support for the debtor. In any case, as a universal principle, the creditor cannot assume a superior position than you with respect to your assets — which means if, for example, your plan does not permit you to withdraw funds before retirement age, your creditor also cannot draw on those funds before you reach retirement. Here are some guidelines to get you thinking about your approach to your retirement accounts.

For one, as mentioned above, do not be in a hurry to rollover your ERISA-qualified plan into an IRA. You should at a minimum check on the law as it applies in your state to see how much coverage you will get. You may have to evaluate the pros and cons, as a self-directed IRA may suit you better than your old employer's ERISA account, or you may find that you are not allowed to leave the money with the employer's plan, but you should make all decisions with due regard to asset protection and also investment and tax planning.

If you have an IRA and are concerned about asset protection because of your state's laws, look into transferring it to an ERISA-qualified plan. You can even create your own plan that can qualify under ERISA. If this idea is appealing, check it out with your financial adviser who will be able to run you through the process.

Later, this book will discuss using foreign trusts to shield your assets, and why his is an option for your IRA, even though it can be expensive and complex. An alternative approach concerns setting up an LLC abroad and transferring the funds, which leaves no money in the United States for creditors to attach. While you can take an advisory role in the investments of the LLC — which could even be back into U.S. investments — you should lose this if you have a judgment pending. The trick is for the foreign LLC to own the funds, and you have no control for recovering the funds outside of the stated company objectives, which would be continued by the manager.

If your IRA is not large and you cannot justify the expense of a complex asset protection plan for it, one alternative can be to liquidate the assets, paying whatever tax penalties are required, and put the money into a straightforward cash shelter, as you would your other funds. While this is somewhat inefficient, if you are facing losing the whole amount, it could still be worthwhile.

A final thought before going beyond the retirement topic and one you might entertain when you consider how well it has worked out for O.J. Simpson to live in Florida, is to move to a state that has better protections in law for both the retirement account and for homesteading. While this is a major step, you may be considering moving anyway, and it does not hurt to investigate beforehand what the particular states legal provisions are to see if it is a good candidate from the asset protection viewpoint.

HOMESTEAD EXEMPTION

The different states vary by the amount of homesteading exemption that they give. The amounts can be as little as $5,000 in Alabama, Georgia, and Kentucky, and unlimited in Florida, as in the case of O.J. Most states have laws that cover between $5,000 and $50,000, which may not seem a good deal in the modern housing climate, despite recent declines in value. There is almost certainly a lot of misunderstanding about how a homestead exemption does or does not shield a home from creditors.

For instance, say you are in a state that provides a $50,000 homestead exemption. Your creditor files a judgment for $200,000 against you, and it happens that your home is worth $200,000.

Your home could be sold at auction to satisfy the judgment, and your creditor would have to first give you $50,000 before taking the rest in part settlement. So, your home is not safe from being sold to satisfy the judgment, as all you have is the amount of the homestead exemption in your hand, which may not buy you another place to live.

But what would happen if you had a mortgage on your home and that mortgage was for $150,000? If the home was sold as before, the creditor would have to give you $50,000 and the mortgage company $150,000; he would have nothing left. In practice, it is unlikely that your creditor would seize the house and force its sale, in other words, it would be protected. Burdening up your house with debt, perhaps by getting a home equity line of credit, is a common way to protect these assets.

What if the creditor is the mortgage company? Unfortunately, nothing works for you then. The homestead exemption does not even apply, and if the home is foreclosed, the lender does not even have to give you $50,000. He just takes the property.

As you might expect, you only get homestead exemption on one property, and that is your home or primary residence. It must be the place you own and occupy as your home; the courts will interpret the state statutes to decide this. Some states might not include a mobile home, even though it is your home. Almost surely, you will have a struggle to prove your primary residence if you live in a less common place such as a houseboat, but Florida has held that a houseboat can comply.

You also have to be careful about your state residency and how long you have owned and occupied the home. Regarding the residency, this would be demonstrated by common factors such as if you have a drivers license, where you pay your taxes, and where your bills are sent, among other things. Notwithstanding all that, you still have to be a resident for a certain time to qualify, and you also need to check into your state's regulations.

Recent amendments to the bankruptcy laws will also limit you. As these are Federal, recall that they take precedence over the state laws. They limit your homestead exemption to a maximum of $125,000 if you purchase your home within 40 months of declaring bankruptcy, regardless of your state's limit. But, this could obviously be less. They also require that you have lived in the state for a minimum of two years. These rules are designed to prevent debtors from last-minute moves to cheat creditors before they file for bankruptcy.

There are other problems with relying on homestead exemptions. In some states, you will need to file a declaration of homestead and cannot assume automatic coverage. Several states forfeit your protection if you title your home to a living trust, yet routinely this is a recommendation from many estate planners to avoid probate. This only goes to show how you must check the impact of every decision on your financial well-being. Also, most homestead laws only protect your home against debts incurred after you have claimed homestead exemption.

Some creditors can override homestead protection and seize the equity in your home. As you might expect, the IRS, being a federal body, can always take your home. It depends on your state's laws whether your home can be seized to pay state taxes. Mortgages or deeds of trust cut straight through the exemption, as noted in the example above, and you will receive nothing from the sale.

The important point to bear in mind is that a homestead exemption is not so powerful in avoiding losing your home to pay your creditors. Even if you think you are covered now because your exemption and your mortgage are worth more than the property, bear in mind that in the normal course of events, houses go up in value year after year, and they will no doubt return to this pattern after the subprime crisis has blown over. Therefore, you might find yourself once again exposed and losing your house for the equity that can be gained from it.

There is one final minor but important point about homestead exemption. Recall the first example, where you owned your house free and clear? It was worth $200,000, and you received $50,000 for your homestead exemption when it was sold at auction. What do you think will happen to that $50,000? It depends on your particular state's statutes, but your creditor could come after that cash to satisfy the judgment. You may have to do something to protect the funds you receive before you lose them. Some states provide no protection for the homestead proceeds, and some do. For example, in California, the proceeds are protected for a period of six months before they can be seized by a creditor.

WAGE EXEMPTION

Now, you ask, can wages be protected to any extent from wage garnishment? We start with the Consumer Credit Protection

Act, which is a Federal statute and limits the amount that can be garnished to 25 percent of your disposable income or the amount by which your disposable income exceeds 30 times the federal minimum hourly wage, whichever is less. The act only protects wages from consumer debt, and not from taxes or business defaults.

Most states follow along with the Federal lines, and some are even more generous in limiting the amount that can be garnished. Note that if the state laws exceed the Federal amounts, and that the Supremacy Laws require that only the Federal amount is withheld. Some states, such as Texas, prohibit wage garnishments absolutely. You should check with your financial adviser to see what applies.

There can be some complications in this. For example, your exempt wages will not be taken by your creditor once you are paid them, provided you keep them separated into a separate account. If you commingle the funds with other money, then you lose that protection.

There are a few ways to try to reduce any wage garnishment. You can reduce it by increasing the withholdings, which reduces your disposable income and results in a tax refund at the end of the year, which is not subject to garnishment. But to eliminate it, you could change the way that you are paid. If you work for someone, the wage garnishment order will tell the employer to not pay you the amount of the garnishment and send it to the creditor. But if you saw it coming, you might set up a company that you would work for, and that company would be paid by your employer. So, when the employer receives the order, he will just ignore it because no one of your name is on the payroll. If you own your own business, you can just go off the payroll and give yourself compensation by means of stock dividends or loans from the company, which would not be subject to the garnishment order.

5

How Well Do You Know Your Business Partners?

"The first mistake in public business is the going into it."
– Benjamin Franklin

Fortunately for the economy, many people choose to ignore Benjamin Franklin's advice, and plummet into starting their own businesses in whatever is their passion or their skill. Whatever it turns out to be, it is more often than not a life-changing event, and the purpose of this chapter is to look at the pros and cons of the simplest forms of business setup. Although there are disadvantages, many people still use these, and by doing so, are often exposing themselves to substantial asset risk.

SOLE PROPRIETORSHIP

The most common form of business ownership and perhaps the most risky in terms of asset protection is a sole proprietorship. This is a simple choice for the individual starting out in business, and examples of sole proprietorship can be found in most sectors of the economy. It may be good for the jewelry store owner or restaurant owner, but is not always the best choice in terms of taxation or lawsuit protection.

Though, as it can be easiest to set up, many business owners opt for this form of business and hope that lawsuits will evade them. I have interviewed several business owners who have opted for this form of ownership. Their best defense seems to rely on the fact that if they give good customer service and do what it takes to keep a customer happy, they will be insulated from lawsuits.

In its simplest of terms, a sole proprietorship is defined as a business owned by one person or the person and his or her spouse. One reason that it is used is that it does not have to be registered with the state as a corporation, limited partnership, or LLC, and there are few formalities involved. This form of business is often the easiest to set up and may be adopted without even knowing it. A freelance writer, a salesman who works on commission, or a contractor who bids on projects may be a sole proprietor.

Yet, even as a sole proprietor, one must always be sure to comply with local, state, and federal regulations. For example, say a jewelry store owner who started advertising his new store in a town before he had obtained all the proper business licenses and tax identification to start his new business. The business owner thought that because he was transferring his business from one location to another that he would be able to get the proper information filed as soon as the business opened. But in a small town, the city collector was not as forgiving and a perfectly good business was almost closed before it ever opened, partly due to poor planning on the business owner's part. The proper information was filed and he turned the potentially bad public relations into lots of good press for his new business, but all could have been avoided if the business owner had thought to research the laws and requirements of the town's business licensing requirements.

The biggest drawback to being a sole proprietor is that the business owner is responsible for all debts owed by the business. If the business owner defaults on a loan or fails to pay a distributor, not only can his or her business and its contents be taken away, but so can the sole proprietor's home, cars, and other personal assets. A sole proprietor is particularly vulnerable for lawsuits.

You do not have to file any special forms or pay any fees to work as a sole proprietor. Though, there may be special licenses you need to file with your city or county you are living in. Most states require even small home-based businesses to register with them and pay a minimum tax. Additionally, you may need to register for an employee identification number (EIN) with the IRS. Sometimes suppliers look to such formalities to assure themselves of the legitimacy of the business before setting up accounts.

Also, if your business is in any other name other than yours, it is frequently necessary to register the fictitious business name with your state. This is because they want to have some indication of who is actually responsible for the business, in case there are any questions or responsibilities to assign. Meeting the tax requirements can be hard for those who own their business as sole proprietorships. IRS data shows that, compared to other taxpayer groups, sole proprietorships have more problems complying with their tax obligations. As a small business owner, you are also responsible for paying Social Security tax and Medicare contributions as a self-employed individual.

GENERAL PARTNERSHIP

As soon as your business starts to grow, if not at the start, you may consider having a friend join in and help you. This automatically stops you from being a sole proprietorship, and you will find, by default, that you are now in a "General Partnership." This is essentially the same as a sole proprietorship, but with more than one person. This has some huge consequences for you.

It is certainly exciting to partner with someone who has complementary strengths, and together, you look to a successful future in your business. You may just shake hands on it while talking it over in a bar, but that is all it takes to legally enter into a partnership with someone. You do not need to sign anything or even have anything written down to be considered a general partnership.

Actually, it is possible that you might have a misunderstanding with your friend and have just been discussing possibilities, when he thinks that you are offering to go into business with him, and actually goes out the next day and starts buying tools and inventory. Such things may even need to be sorted out in front of the judge, who must decide on the basis of who he believes. Of course, it is only likely to come in front of a judge if there are problems, and the camaraderie with which it started suddenly evaporates.

You may think that this is an unlikely scenario, but consider, as we all do, discussing interesting and unique ideas that might be profitable with your friend. Where is the line between avid enthusiasm and what you should actually do separated from what you said you were going to do? There are always flashes of what it takes to be brilliant in everyone's minds, but when it is suddenly realized, there could be a market for your latest brainwave. But, if you make plans over a few beers, you could always find yourself taking on much more than you intended.

You might not intend for a partnership to exist, but what about your only employee coming up with a solid idea to double your sales? It is not unknown for people to feel that they have earned a partnership in the business by making significant contributions. That point is sometimes argued in the courts.

Of course, sometimes you should be aware that you are forming a partnership. For instance, if you buy an investment property with a friend and both your names are put on the title, that can have significant hidden risks, as your share of the assets is vulnerable.

Before the downside is discussed, take a look at the advantages of the general partnership. These are, in essence, the same as a sole proprietorship, in that you do not have to do anything special to establish it and there are no statutory requirements about decision-making. They are simple and cheap; you only have to do the ordinary accounting procedures that you would want to for any business. You do not even have to file any annual reports. For tax purposes, the general partnership is a pass-through entity, which means the profits and losses are not taxed on the partnership, but go through to the individual partners' tax returns as income. If there were unequal contributions to the partnership, then the profits would normally be divided in the same way.

Sounds terrific, does it not? There is none of that formality or form filling, and you can spend all your energies on developing the business. A general partnership is the most dangerous business vehicle that you can have from an asset protection viewpoint and should be avoided at just about all costs. You should not believe anyone who tells you that you need to have a general partnership for any particular business, as one of the alternatives is bound to be applicable and superior. The only benefit for the general partnership, in effect, is the ease of doing it, and that should be the only excuse for anyone to unwittingly enter into one.

The root of the problem with any general partnership is that any of the partners is responsible for any other partner's actions and any claims. Every partner is considered to be an agent of the partnership, and can legally bind the entire partnership and the partners. That is why I asked in the heading how well you know your partners — if they could do anything that you would not, you are not going to be happy.

Actually, to put it more bluntly, all general partners are personally liable to an unlimited extent for any act or omission of any other partner, and liable for all liabilities and accidents from the partnership. A creditor trying to collect on a partnership debt can, and will, go after the deepest pocket. Even if the richest partner thought that he was putting up the finance as a sleeping partner, leaving the other partners to work and run the business, he can be pursued for 100 percent of the debt. There is no escape by claiming, or even proving, that you knew nothing about what one of your partners was doing in the name of the partnership — even if you were vacationing far away at the time.

As an example, say you get together with four other friends and buy an apartment building as an investment property, sharing the running costs and the rents while hoping to make some appreciation on your capital. You did not do anything special and you are a joint owner, so by default you are in a general partnership. Things are not going too well, but your partner, John, decides to re-carpet the whole building. Unfortunately, he did not tell anyone else, and your partnership cannot afford the bill. If you have been following along so far, you perhaps realize that between the four of you, you have to pay anyway. If you do not, then any and all of you can be sued, and as a result, the carpet company gets their money.

You say, "I will learn from that experience." When you decide to buy another apartment building with just three partners because none of you want to work with John, you prepare a partnership agreement which appoints you as the managing general partner with sole authority to make purchases and sign legal documents for the partnership. Things are going well until Mark decides that the building needs painting and puts in the order. He did not ask you. If he had, he would have found out that the partnership has little cash available because of the re-plumbing you had to have done earlier in the year. The painting job puts you into the red again. Do you have to pay it?

Absolutely, despite the agreement. A general partner legally has the "apparent authority" to commit the partnership — in other words, it is not up to the painters to check whether Mark has a right to sign for the partnership. Again, you can all be sued if you do not pay. Of course, you might have a case to sue Mark later, as he ignored the partnership agreement. I think you can see why a general partnership is one of the most dangerous things that you can do for asset protection. It can only get better from here.

LIMITED PARTNERSHIP

While a general partnership is often a disaster, a limited partnership is extremely different. A general partnership can happen even before you know it, and that is not the case with a limited partnership. You have to intend to form a limited partnership, and to do so, you have to comply with the requirements of your state's Limited Partnership Act, which is enacted in every state except Louisiana. You have to fill out the forms and file with the Secretary of State, paying the appropriate amount and naming someone as the statutory agent in case the partnership is sued. That way, it is similar to having a company or corporation.

The big difference is that, unlike a general partnership, the limited partners do not have to participate in the day-to-day activities of the partnership, and they also do not have personal liability for the debts and obligations of the partnership. It is still a pass-through entity for tax purposes and actually, the profits and losses can be allocated in any way you want, regardless of each partner's investment. It is a business structure that is suited to people who want to attract investors, without handing over any decision-making powers. All the limited partners can never be held liable for any debts of the business, which makes it good for attracting investors who would avoid a general partnership. All the limited partners have at risk is the amount of money they have invested in the business.

While the limited partners do not in actuality have any rights in managing the business, most states give them the rights necessary to protect their interests by examining the books and other limited things. This way, the limited partnership is similar to being a shareholder of a corporation. Limited partners cannot bind the partnership in any way or sign a contract for the partnership. If they try to, they could legally take on the mantle of another general partner and lose the asset protection they wish to enjoy.

At this point, it is important to note that there is one exception to the absolute lack of liability for the business debts. This is called "piercing the corporate veil" — whether it applies to companies or partnerships — and this danger comes if the partners can be shown to be ignoring their own partnership and acting in general association rather than obeying the rules for the partnership by having meetings, for example, as required. The argument runs that if the partners can ignore their own partnership, then a creditor may also ignore it and seek compensation from the personal assets of the limited partners. So, for instance, the partnership should keep separate accounts and hold a separate bank account as a minimum to show its existence is real and not just a liability dodging convenience.

Yet, each limited partnership has to have at least one general partner, and many only have the one. The general partner, in the same way as in a general partnership, has the responsibilities and liabilities for the business, so at first sight, this is still a lousy position to hold. The general partner has authority to bind the partnership legally and is personally liable for all of the partnership's debts. Any creditor can go after the general partner's personal assets to satisfy a partnership liability.

The way around this, and to provide some asset protection, is based in the fact that partners in a limited partnership do not have to be real people, but could be a corporation, a trust, or another partnership. If a general partner is a corporation, for instance, you will get the protections that apply to a corporation, which you will learn about later.

Considering just the entities that we have discussed so far, another form of protection would be for the general partner to set up a limited partnership to which they transferred all their assets and real estate, among other things. This would require duties like re-titling the real estate and stock certificates. Although transferring goods sometimes attracts capital gains taxes, it should not in this case, as the tax code exempts the transfer of appreciated assets to a partnership, with minor exceptions. It is important to note that you should be a limited partner in this new partnership, with perhaps your spouse as the general partner.

Now consider what happens if the original business partnership has a problem and is sued. The limited partners are all right, apart from possibly losing their investments in the business, as long as the business of the limited partnership has been properly conducted. The focus of the lawsuit is the general partner.

As is common in these cases, you, as the general partner, are subpoenaed to appear in the court and answer questions about your assets. This is a crucial event, and there is no way to hide the truth — it is an incredibly serious business if you lie, but you do not have to if you have structured your affairs properly. If the creditors ask you if you own any real estate, you do not; it is in your other partnership's name. If they ask you if you own stocks, again the truthful answer is negative. The creditors may even ask if you own any partnership assets — in this case, you must answer yes. But the creditors are not able to get at those assets, as you are only a limited partner in the protective partnership, and there is no direct line to the assets. This protective partnership has done nothing wrong and cannot be sued to satisfy the judgment against the business partnership.

Does this all seem too easy? Well, there are one or two points to consider. The creditors can try to get at your interest in the second partnership by getting what is called a "charging order" against it. The rules of the Limited Partnership Act allow that creditors can charge the partnership interest of the partner with payment. The effect of this is to make the creditor able to get the partner's distributions of any partnership income. That is all that is available to them — they cannot force the partnership to dissolve and get at the partnership's assets, as you are only a limited partner. Actually, because the general partner of the second partnership is friendly to you — or, at least, is your spouse — they can decide that there are no distributions to be made, so the charging order will receive nothing.

All this is hard on the creditor, but is one of the ways in which you can achieve some asset protection. The idea behind this limitation on the creditors is that to allow them to break up a partnership to satisfy the debts of one partner would be unfair to the innocent partners. The compromise is that the creditor gets the payouts that the partner would get, and this does not disrupt the business of the partnership. Actually, in Florida and Arizona, this limitation is spelled out in the law, making the charging order the only remedy available. Other states have established the same thing by precedent in the courts.

In reality, if the general partner is a friend of the limited partner, it is quite common that no dividends will be paid if a charging order exists. There is nothing that requires the general partner to issue regular dividends, and it is plainly not in the interests of the limited partner. Although we are getting to the finer points here, it is possible for the limited partner still to receive some money from the partnership, for specific tasks undertaken, say as a consultant. The creditor can call this course of action into question, though.

There is also a fascinating trick that allows you to provide a disincentive for creditors. This requires that the partnership declares a profit and distribution, and for the sake of business development decides that the funds need to stay within the partnership and be reinvested. Each partner would then be liable for the taxes, as if they had received the money, and would typically have to find the funds from some other venture, or from savings. Now when the creditor steps into your shoes, he can find himself in this position. There is a notional dividend, which requires taxes to be paid, but no money will be handed out. Consequently, it actually costs the creditor money for tax payments to take out a charging order against your position.

FAMILY LIMITED PARTNERSHIP

While we are talking about the general and limited partners being friends, I should mention the topic of the family limited partnership. You may have heard of this term and wondered in what way it was special. The fact is that a family limited partnership is simply a limited partnership that you establish with members of your family and as such, is subject to all the points previously discussed. This has for many years been a popular way for families to create wealth preservation plans and ensure continuous succession of assets to future generations.

The most frequently used arrangement is for the husband and wife to be both general and limited partners in the limited partnership; it is quite permissible for one person to hold both positions. They would contribute their income producing assets to the partnership, which are the ones that are most effectively covered by a limited partnership. As general partners, they would have only a small interest, but their limited partner personas would hold a majority interest. Now, their assets would be protected from creditors.

In time, they could gradually gift their limited partner interests to their children. One of the advantages of the family limited partnership is the way that you can spread the tax burden between the partners as you choose. For example, the main wage earner could contribute large amounts to the partnership, but only have a small interest. As a general partner, he would still have full control, but this ploy would spread the tax burden to the other partners, such as the children, who hold a large interest in the partnership.

As for family limited partnerships; you should be careful before putting your home under the ownership of the partnership. Possibilities will be discussed later for your home ownership to provide asset protection. You should understand that you may lose your tax advantages, such as mortgage interest relief, if you take title into the partnership.

In conjunction with a family limited partnership, often you may have a living trust holding the limited partnership interests, which allows them to be bequeathed, avoiding probate. Also, the general partner could be a corporation or a LLC controlled by the husband and wife, which would enable greater avoidance of liability. Corporations and LLCs will be discussed in the following chapters.

6

Surely Incorporation Is for Big Companies?

"A criminal is a person with predatory instincts who has not sufficient capital to form a corporation."
– Howard Scott

oving on from partnerships, the next business structure to consider is the corporation. The limited liability that you enjoy with a corporation is not from statute or case law; it arises from the idea that the corporation is an entirely separate entity from the individuals who own it, or its shareholders. It is, in effect, another person, with powers to sue and be sued, among other things. This is why it has no direct effect on your personal assets when the corporation is in debt — you are only liable for the amount that you have put into it — your share.

CORPORATION CREATION

A corporation is formed by filing articles of incorporation with the state. In return, the state will grant you your charter. You will need to choose a name which is not the same as one already in use, or too similar. You may find some online resources help you to determine this. Actually, in many states, you can reserve your name online while you are sending in your forms. Of course, your state may allow your name, but you may find it is similar to a company in a different state, or infringes a trademark, so an online search is the least you should do to check on this.

When you file, you will need to give the name and address of the statutory agent, as before, who is the person who is a legal representative to whom a summons can be issued against the corporation. You also used to give a description of the purpose of the corporation, but that practice has now been done away with. I say thankfully, because if the corporation was found to be doing something that was not listed, it was deemed to be an ultra vires act, and this negated the limited liability of the corporation. In effect, if it was not listed, the corporation could not be doing it, so the shareholders were assumed to have done it acting as individuals.

Once you file and have been accepted, the corporation can continue forever. As it is not tied to any particular person, it does not cease on anyone's death, and if the fees and taxes continue to be paid, then the state will continue to recognize it. It can only be eliminated by taking the step of liquidation. Of course, as in the previous chapter, there can be the legal instance of "penetrating the corporate veil" if you do not run the corporation in a business-like manner, keeping good records, and maintaining separate accounts.

If you are running a business as a sole proprietor or in general partnership, you should seriously consider incorporating your business right away for the protection that it offers. But you will want to read future chapters to determine the best choice for your situation. Bear in mind that, no matter how small your business, you are never safe from a lawsuit, hence you need to increase the protection that you have. You do not have to do anything wrong in particular; for example, if you sold goods which were manufactured badly, then your customer would sue you for any injuries resulting from their use – the lawsuit may also reach the manufacturer, but you would like to know that you are secure from such claims, right?

S-CORPORATION

There are two main types of corporation, the S-corporation and the C-corporation. Which type of corporation you select has a big effect on your taxation. Often, the S-corporation is recommended because the C-corporation is directly taxed. The S-corporation is a corporation that has elected to be treated for tax under subchapter S of the internal revenue code. This means it is a pass-through tax entity and the corporation does not pay tax directly. Because it is a corporation, you still get asset protection.

Individual taxpayers pay tax on their share of the profits and have to declare them on their tax returns. There is a trap here for the unwary. You pay tax on your share of the profits, which are divided proportionately. You do not necessarily pay tax on the amount of money you receive. If, for instance, the shareholders determined that they should keep the money in the business account for future expansion, they would still have to pay taxes as if they had received the money. This is called "phantom income," and it is quite common with S-corporations. You just have to find the money to pay the taxes somewhere else.

There are strict rules on who can be members of an S-corporation. You are limited to 75 shareholders, and all the shareholders must be U.S. citizens or legal residents. None of the shareholders can be another business, partnership, or organization, and you also cannot include even one foreign shareholder. You are also expected to be an operating business and not just a holding company.

There is another way that the S-corporation is tax efficient. Any business is charged 15.3 percent self-employment tax on any earned income, and that is what a sole proprietorship or general partnership would have to pay. Yet, operating as an S-corporation, you can decide to take some of the income as a salary and some as business profits. You would only be charged the self-employment tax on the salary portion. The IRS requires that you take a reasonable salary but does not go on to define what this means. Obviously, the lower the salary, the less you lose in self-employment tax. The test of a reasonable salary is in reality what you would earn doing a similar job working for someone else, and provided you keep this within the bounds of commonsense, you can save some more money.

C-CORPORATION

With all that said, the most common type of corporation is the C-corporation. This type is almost universal for the big companies. Any benefits there are with the C-corporation are quite limited for a small business, unless you intend going public one day. Ownership of stock can be freely traded without having to get other shareholders' approval, and that is essential in a publicly traded company. Some of the advantages espoused for a C-corporation are the tax deductions that you can have, such as medical costs, cafeteria plans, life insurance, and tuition reimbursement, just to name a few. Though, if you do the math, you will more often than not find that these are not a sufficient advantage in a small business.

Against that, you have to set the fact that the corporation is taxed as a separate entity, at a rate of 15 percent for the first $50,000. The shareholders' dividends are also taxed. This is the well-known double taxation trap. It is commonly not an advantage for a small business to be organized as a C-corporation. It is only truly appropriate if you need the ability for the public to buy shares, giving easy transferability of ownership, or for certain types of businesses, such as banks and insurance companies, where it is required by law.

CORPORATION ORGANIZATION

To be able to make a choice, you need to know how the corporation is organized. Whether the corporation is public or private, it has a similar configuration. You have three groups of people: the shareholders, who own the company; the directors, who legally operate the company; and the officers, who are in the day-to-day management of the company and are also employees.

As the owners, ultimately the shareholders (also called stockholders), are in control. Yet, they are not normally expected to deal with the day-to-day running of the company, unless they also happen to hold another position in the corporation.

The shareholders are entitled to share the profits each year, divided up according to their share of business. These are the dividends that are issued by large companies. With a small business, often no dividends are issued to avoid the double taxation. Instead, the earnings are distributed as compensation which is deductible to the corporation, or the corporation seeks to qualify as an S-corporation. The only proviso is that the compensation must be a reasonable amount for work performed.

As the owners, the shareholders have control by and large of the business and elect the directors. Depending on the state law, you may be able to change directors at any time, or you may have to wait until the annual general meeting to replace the board of directors. If you are a majority shareholder, with more than 50 percent of the shares, your decision on this will usually be absolute. More often than not, no one shareholder has control, so such actions come down to a majority decision.

If the company does not pay dividends, the effect of owning 51 percent of the shares is the same as owning 99 percent, under this system. And if you only have 49 percent of the shares, you can never force your point of view. But there is a thing called cumulative voting, which is used in some states. It is required by the California Corporations Code, for instance, and permitted in New York and Illinois, but does not have to be used if the majority of the shareholders vote it out. Its use helps to preserve minority shareholder representation, instead of the situation above, where 49 percent will never be heard.

With cumulative voting, each share has as many votes as there are vacancies to be voted on. Though, you can put all your votes toward one candidate. For instance, with 500 shares and four vacancies, you have 2,000 votes that you can give to one candidate, or you can give 1,000 votes to each of two candidates, as opposed to giving 500 votes to a candidate for each of the vacancies. This allows even minority shareholders a better say in the election, and also less frustration with never being able to put your point of view in a meaningful way.

The directors are legally responsible for operating the business and meet at regular intervals to discuss this. They are legally required to have an annual general meeting, which is when the shareholders can have their say. They appoint the officers of the company, which include the president, vice president, corporate secretary, treasurer, and others as they wish. The officers do the day-to-day running and receive salaries in return.

Just because you have a corporation does not mean you can never have personal liability for the corporate debts. If the business incurred liabilities before it was incorporated, then the business owners would still be personally liable, depending on the formation that they were operating under.

Much will also depend on the size of the corporation. Obviously, a mainstream business is creditworthy and can borrow from a bank with little difficulty. But if you have a small business, even if it is incorporated, you may be asked to give a personal guarantee against any loans. This is only the bank being prudent because the business does not have the track record that they would look for.

This does not mean that every owner/shareholder would have to sign for the total amount to be borrowed. As with all things, this can be negotiated, and the bank may accept each owner only signing for his or her share of the debt. A common provision that many banks try to include is an option to accelerate the loan if one of the guarantors dies. If possible, this should be negotiated out.

There are also some statutory exceptions to the lack of personal liability. The most common of these is that the IRS can hold any responsible person liable for taxes that are being withheld from wages, but not submitted to them. If things are going badly, this is quite a common way for the business to try and stay afloat. It is much more likely that the rent and utilities will be paid, and that wages will also be paid, and if there is not enough money to go around, the tax man will (temporarily) lose out. For the purposes of this statute, they can hold directors and officers personally liable, and also any controlling majority shareholder. The standard for whether this sticks is quite low and amounts to knowing that the withholdings were not sent to the IRS. They can even get to you if you should have known, but were so derelict in your duties that you were unaware.

On the other hand, if the corporate taxes are not paid, the IRS normally cannot go after you. This is because the business counts as a separate person, and there is no provision in the internal revenue code to change this perception.

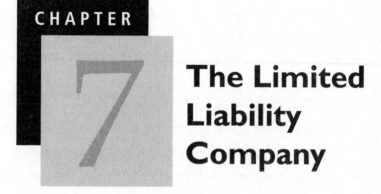

CHAPTER 7

The Limited Liability Company

"Corporation, n. An ingenious device for obtaining individual profit without individual responsibility."
– Ambrose Bierce

We have now considered several forms of business ownership, and come up with some ideas for asset protection. There is one more form of company that is a fairly recent invention, which many people find is the best answer for their business. It is called the limited liability company, or LLC.

BUSINESS OWNERSHIP REVIEW

We have considered all the ways you can own a business. The first is sole proprietorship, which is the worst you can have for asset protection. You are exposed just as a simple person to all the liability consequences of the business, and your business is exposed to your personal liabilities. If you are in business with someone else, you have all the choices that I have detailed so far.

The general partnership is an asset protection disaster. On the bright side, it is a pass-through tax entity, so you do not have double taxation. You have flexibility in how you arrange your share of the business. But it is dangerous not just for your own actions, but also because you pick up liability for the actions of all your partners.

The limited partnership largely overcomes the limitations of the general partnership, with the exception of the general partner, who is just as exposed to all lawsuits and creditors. You can adjust your deductions and credits just as with a general partnership, and this business can work out well for the limited partners. The issue of who will be the general partner is the tricky one.

We then discussed corporations, in particular the S-corporation and C-corporation. Because of their arrangement as separate personas, these provide good asset protection, but at the expense of flexibility compared with the partnerships, and there is more paperwork involved in forming and keeping them up.

The S-corporation is the best for tax avoidance, as long as you can maintain the conditions to keep this status. If you get one non-resident alien or a corporate shareholder, then you cannot keep the pass-through tax status. And then the C-corporation has the problem of double taxation, along with all the paperwork.

So all of these business organizations have disadvantages, even though they can be worked around when you appreciate the shortcomings. Actually, it is quite likely that your ideal asset protection and tax avoidance plan could include one or more of them, in a multiple entity formation.

LIMITED LIABILITY COMPANY

As a result of all these entities having limitations and disadvantages, a new legal entity sprang up in 1977 in Wyoming, and has now spread across the states. The LLC came out of a need for mining developers to attract foreign investors, and includes a limited liability in a partnership type arrangement. In other words, the LLC gives you the option of single taxation, the members being taxed on the LLC's profits, and the LLC as such paying no taxes. Actually, the members can vote on how their tax is treated and structure deductions as they wish, allowing the LLC to be used in a flexible way.

Every state now has legislation enabling LLCs, although it is not so standardized as, for example, the limited partnership legislation, and some issues are still being resolved in courts as cases come up. This is why you may find certain attorneys still a little resistant to recommend them. The LLC has members, rather than partners or shareholders, and the members' interests are protected, with only the charging order remedy available to creditors. There are no restrictions on who can be a member, allowing foreign and corporate bodies to qualify, unlike the S-corporation. Also, unlike limited partners, the members can take part in the management without losing their limited liability.

The other term used with LLCs is manager, which is equivalent to the general partner in partnerships but without the liability. You do not actually have to have a manager, and you can have more than one, and, either way, there is no personal liability for the debts of the LLC.

David Tanzer has extensive experience in the asset protection field, and includes LLCs in his case study example.

CASE STUDY: DAVID A TANZER

Over thirty years in law and business, David Tanzer concentrates in international planning for clients located around the world. Tanzer provides guidance to individuals and businesses, assisting them in mitigating personal and business risks, allowing for opportunities for wealth preservation, asset protection, financial growth and pre-migration planning. A former Judge, retired commercial litigation attorney, and an Adjunct Professor of International Law in the U.S. and Australia, Tanzer places emphasis on advance planning steps before a problem materializes.

David Tanzer is a member of the Offshore Institute, a multidisciplinary international professional organization of individuals engaged in offshore and international planning. David is on the Wealth Advisory Panel of the Oxford Club, a private, international organization of investors and entrepreneurs.

Appointed to the bench of the Circuit Court of Cook County, Illinois as Chairman Judicial Arbitration Panel, David has tried complex civil cases, developing special expertise in business and transactional law, commercial litigation, asset protection and wealth preservation. After entering private law practice he became a named partner in the law firm of Bjork, Tanzer & Associates, Ltd., in Chicago, Illinois, and then establishing the law firm David A. Tanzer & Associates, P.C., in Vail, Colorado.

Tanzer has also been a member of the Colorado Bar Association Judiciary Executive Counsel, the American Bar Association, Chicago Bar Association, Northwest Bar Association, Association of Trial Lawyers of America, and the Continental Divide Bar Association. He is also an Associate Member of the Auckland District Law Society, New Zealand - Foreign Lawyer, and an Associate Member of the Queensland Law Society, Australia - Foreign Lawyer.

CASE STUDY: DAVID A TANZER

The author of the books **How to Legally Protect Your Assets and Offshore Living & Investing**, and numerous articles on international business and asset protection planning, David Tanzer is a sought after speaker on topics of international asset protection planning and wealth preservation.

David A Tanzer, David A. Tanzer & Associates, P.C.
2121 N. Frontage Rd. W. # 209
Vail, CO 81657
Tel. 970-476-6100 • Fax. 720-293-2272
Datlegal@aol.com or Dat@DavidTanzer.com
www.DavidTanzer.com

In what way are you involved with asset protection, and does this include general estate planning and tax issues?

100 percent of my professional time is involved in asset protection. I started working with international planning techniques around 1990. At that time you could count those of us doing work in this area on one hand and have several fingers left over. Asset protection should always integrate estate planning into the overall structure.

Only two decades ago, asset protection planning was often done in isolation and without regard to the overall life and death cycle of clients. Originally, the focus was on protecting the assets of high risk individuals. However, planning has evolved and now includes both the life side and the aging and death side of protecting and preserving assets. Integrating all segments into one overall plan makes good sense. Planning for only one or the other is missing the big picture.

Next, understand that your estate plan should address the concerns of potentially huge estate taxes which may be assessed upon the transfer of your assets when you die. The good news is that you can substantially reduce your estate taxes if allowable credits and proper estate planning techniques are used effectively. However, it is essential for your estate planners and advisers to work closely together to legally reduce your taxable estate.

CASE STUDY: DAVID A TANZER

In the U.S., there are both federal and state guidelines that must be closely followed. And prepare your estate plan with a current financial statement of all assets and their values, relying upon qualified individuals to assist you in establishing and realizing your goals.

Remember that good estate planning consists of both proper documentation and implementation. One without the other is not enough. A good estate plan includes the retitling of assets, transferring ownership of assets, renaming beneficiaries of life insurance and retirement benefits, and many, many other details that must be taken into account.

The list of techniques for estate tax savings tools is a long one. Too often, I have seen a high asset client walk into my office without even the basic, organized estate plan to really assist with asset preservation, even though a Will and a trust might exist. Often, a long time attorney-friend helped put together their estate plan and they assumed their house was in order in the event of untimely death. Is death ever timely?

Do you specialize in any particular aspects of asset protection, such as foreign trusts or LLCs?

Yes — in business and personal asset protection planning, some people wish to protect assets domestically, while maintaining income tax and economic neutrality. One way of doing this is through the combination of a tax neutral domestic "asset protection trust" and one or more LLC.

By way of example, let's first place your business in one LLC called the "Business LLC" and your after tax cash, stocks and mutual fund assets (the cash) into another LLC which we'll call your "Nest Egg" LLC. You are the manager of both and make all investment and business decisions.

Importantly, different LLC jurisdictions and statutory provisions result in very different LLC protection. Some are very marginal indeed, and others offering Charging Order protection as a sole remedy are superior. The content of the

CASE STUDY: DAVID A TANZER

LLC Operating Agreement and the ancillary documentation also greatly affect the results.

Next, instead of you owning the LLC membership interests, let's place them into an asset protection trust. Best of all, an International Trust there is an important distinction between domestic and offshore trusts, and offshore trusts offer superior asset protection. But for now, you place the LLC interests into a trust. Instead of you owning the membership interests, the trust owns them.

Depending on the type of trust, revocable or irrevocable, where it is registered, and many other factors, the level of protection afforded to the LLC membership interests may become substantially enhanced. What's more, the trust may maintain Charging Order protection with the proper establishment of the LLC. There are many types of LLCs and trusts, and many will offer no or limited protection. By creating a trust that avails itself to asset protective provisions and integrating it with a properly established LLC, you can enhance asset protection significantly.

Before you run out and set up your own LLC, remember that all LLCs are not created equally. Different jurisdictions offer very different protection. The Operating Agreement and other formalities must be set up in a manner to provide the best opportunity to achieve protection. And too, you must use great caution before transferring personal assets into an LLC to avoid negative tax consequences.

For now, this is the basic concept.

There are numerous ways to hold and own LLC membership interests. One excellent option would be to place 99 percent LLC interests in an International Trust. The result is you only personally own 1 percent interest, equal to only 1% of the total value of the assets in the LLC. Accordingly, your personal risk exposure is now limited to 1% of the value of these assets.

CASE STUDY: DAVID A TANZER

Segregating asset risk classes and limiting values within different entities are basic goals. For example, placing lower risk assets like cash, stocks and bonds into a "Nest Egg" LLC would be separate from a Business LLC which generates higher risk.

If you transfer your principal residence into an LLC, it should be a single member LLC. This means it is 100 percent trust owned. The LLC then elects to be treated as a disregarded entity for tax purposes. This presents opportunities to maintain the $500,000 husband-wife capital gains exemption upon the sale of the home, which has been a matter of dispute in the legal and tax communities for some time. However, the IRS provided guidance on the classification of qualified entities of a home owned by a husband and wife in Rev. Proc. 2002-69. With the trust also being treated as a disregarded entity for U.S. domestic tax purposes, it logically follows that this is the preferred method to hold title to your principal residence.

Thus far we have discussed three new entities, two LLCs, one owned 99 percent by the trust and 1 percent by you, the other 100 percent owned by the trust, and the International Trust. You have also retitled, or conveyed, your assets into the LLCs. The assets are the same assets as before, located at the same local bank. You have not relocated or transferred your assets to distant parts of the world. You control the assets in the LLC as the manager. And as the Protector of the trust, you exercise control over the trust and trustees.

And there is much more we can do in expanding the above basic concept.

Do you find that a single entity or strategy is sufficient for most people, or do you commonly recommend a multi-layered structure?

Asset protection is always customized to the needs of individuals. Structuring, per se, is not a hallmark of quality asset protection, only an example of planning for some individuals…. nothing more. Sometimes a single entity may be sufficient, but for more active businesses and professional clients, a multi-layered strategy is generally superior.

CASE STUDY: DAVID A TANZER

Have you found that you have needed to change your methods in recent years, because of FTC v. Affordable Media, or to include Nevis LLCs?

The Anderson case (as it is known) is a good example of bad planning. We have never created plans of the type and style of Anderson, so we have never needed to change our planning as a result of Anderson.

In a highly controversial case originating in Nevada during the late 1990s, a couple dealt with the very issue of maintaining too much control over an offshore trust after a judgment was taken against them. The case was highly publicized and became known as the "Anderson" case (F.T.C. v. Affordable Media, LLC, et al, 179 F.3d 1228 (9th Cir. 1999), 1999 U.S. App. Lexis 13130). This case, even though arguably rife with bad facts throughout, sets forth an important lesson in how not to set up a trust and respond to court orders.

The Andersons were involved in a very successful and profitable Ponzi Scheme, where the payment of profits to early investors was only available based upon money paid into the scam by later investors. Their actions were held to be illegal by the judge, based upon fraud. Millions of dollars poured in, which the U.S. government claimed was hidden with the assistance of a trust registered in the Cook Islands. The Federal Trade Commission (FTC) acted to shut them down and have monies returned to the U.S. Then a suit was filed in Nevada, and the local judge ordered the Andersons to return all monies to Nevada.

The Andersons acted as both the domestic trustee and the Protector of the trust so they could continue to retain full power and control over it. This is certainly not a practice I would ever recommend, for reasons you will soon see. And only after the judge ordered them to repatriate the money back into the U.S., did the Andersons resign as the domestic trustees of the trust.

Furthermore, they also continued, at least initially, to act as Protectors. The Andersons sent instructions to the foreign trustee in the Cook Islands to return the money, pursuant to the judge's order. The foreign trustee, acting according to the anti-duress terms of the trust, properly refused to repatriate monies.

CASE STUDY: DAVID A TANZER

The Andersons then argued to the judge that they followed the court order but the foreign trustee failed to return any assets. Their defense was based upon the Doctrine of Impossibility, since the trustee refused to repatriate the funds (due to an anti-duress clause) and it was therefore impossible to comply with the order of the court. The court noted that the Andersons were originally the domestic trustees when the order was issued, and they retained the power as Protectors to determine what events were duress. The judge then ordered the Andersons to jail until they complied with the order of court. In other words, the return of the money was not impossible but for the events the Andersons themselves created. The Andersons only resigned as Protectors after they sat in jail for refusing to comply with the judge's order.

In the meantime, the FTC filed suit in the Cook Islands for the return of the money, based upon the U.S. judgment against the Andersons. The foreign trustee of the trust in the Cook Islands defended the suit pursuant to the terms of the trust. The court in the Cook Islands not only denied the claim of the FTC pursuant to the terms of the trust and the Cook Island laws, but the judge charged the FTC with paying the Anderson's court costs and expenses, including attorney's fees, in defending the suit that it considered improper. A favorable result in the Cook Islands for the Andersons, indeed.

The Andersons, in the meantime, were released from jail because they could not possibly comply with the order of the court, as they were no longer the domestic trustees or the Protectors. All said and done, the money remained intact in the trust established by the Andersons, and the Andersons are freely out and about.

The assets remained intact in the Anderson's trust in the Cook Islands. No funds have ever been repatriated by order of court. However, it is understood that the Andersons did eventually settle the case with the FTC for a fraction of the claim.

CASE STUDY: DAVID A TANZER

Briefly describe a "success" story, that is, an asset protection plan that was threatened in some way and withstood the attack, and why. Please change names as you think fit.

Mr. Martin owned a successful lounge and restaurant business at the bottom of the ski slopes in Aspen, CO, known for outstanding après ski called The Spot. Après ski is defined as a gathering time following a great day on the ski mountain where you can indulge in food and drink and meet some of those interesting bodies you saw skiing past you during the day.

The Martins, a young couple with two small children, were worth several million dollars. His wife, Dr. Martin, was a physician in the community, working part-time at two medical offices as an independent subcontractor. They had good prospects of increasing their wealth in the future due to appreciation of assets and conservative management objectives. Mr. Martin started The Spot about a decade ago, and it literally turned into a cash cow. Dr. Martin made a comfortable salary. Instead of living lavishly and consuming wildly, they invested their income wisely, owning eight different commercial and residential investment properties, and a comfortable nest egg.

Mr. Martin's greatest concern was the ongoing liability from the bar and commercial rental properties. Dr. Martin's professional liability risks were her concern. The business was set up in a corporation, which was not up to date with compliance and formalities. They had no asset protection strategy and they were justifiably concerned that one mishap could wipe out their assets.

The Spot was estimated to be worth approximately $1 million and in an S-Corp without any business debt. The couple jointly owned their home, valued at $900,000 with a $400,000 mortgage and $500,000 in equity. The real estate investments had equity ranging in value between $30,000 and $500,000; two were residential, and the others were commercial properties. They held $30,000 in cash, $150,000 in stocks, $100,000 in bonds, and $200,000 in deferred income (IRAs and pension plans). They owned personal property worth approximately $125,000.

CASE STUDY: DAVID A TANZER

After discussing tax issues related to The Spot and the investment properties, and a review of personal goals for Mr. & Dr. Martin and the family, an International Trust structure was created. There were numerous viable options for protecting the Martin's assets.

First, a Nest Egg LLC was established. The cash, C-Corp stock, and bonds, and personal property were placed into this LLC. The deferred income accounts were left in their own names, since transferring these assets into the structure would create negative tax consequences. The transfer would trigger taxes on the IRAs and pension plan monies, and early withdrawal penalties would occur. The Martins were aware that once they reached retirement age and withdrew from the deferred income accounts, these monies could then be placed into the Nest Egg LLC. The total to the Nest Egg LLC was $280,000.

All of the cash personally owned in the money market funds and in the stock and bond accounts were transferred into the name of the Nest Egg LLC. New account numbers were assigned, but they continued to hold the cash, stocks and bonds at the same place they were held prior to the transfer. The Nest Egg LLC was the new owner of these assets, and the accounts were held in the name of the LLC.

The Martins were the managers of the Nest Egg LLC, retaining control over all assets transferred into it. They owned 1 percent interest in the LLC, and 99% interest was to be transferred into and owned by a trust. When the Martins needed to deposit or withdraw funds from these accounts in the future, they would do so exactly as they had in the past, except acting as the manager of the LLC. Distribution agreements were also created so the Martins had the option of withdrawing up to $150,000 per year from the LLC without further formalities.

The home was transferred into the Home LLC, which was owned 100 percent by the trust — a single member LLC. They had built up considerable value in the home during the past decade and desired to maintain the husband and wife $500,000 capital gains tax exception.

Placing the home into its own LLC isolated it from all other assets, should a dispute arise from an event not related to the home. Both of the Martins were managers of the Home LLC.

After a review of the investment real estate assets, we isolated them by risk and equity values. The two residential apartments, one with $30,000 in equity and another with $75,000 in equity, were both transferred into Res LLC. The Martins were willing to accept the risk that might arise from the lower equity property exposing the larger equity property, but they sought to minimize LLC structures and cost.

The commercial investment real estate was next. Commercial property with $100,000 in equity was transferred into Com No. 1 LLC, the commercial property with $150,000 into Com No. 2 LLC. The Martins considered transferring both properties into one LLC for purposes of minimizing the number of LLCs and costs, but decided against it because they understood commercial property was a higher-risk asset than residential property. Each of the remaining four commercial properties with equity values between $200,000 and $500,000 were transferred into Com No. 3 LLC, Com No. 4 LLC, Com #5 LLC and Com No. 6 LLC.

For tax purposes, income and expenses for each investment real estate LLC would be calculated and passed through on IRS Tax Form 1120s to the trust. Then, it was again passed through the trust on an informational tax return on Tax Form 1041 and on to the Martins on their personal tax returns. They would continue to maintain all tax benefits of owning the investment property.

The Spot nightclub was handled differently. It was already in an S-Corp. owned by Mr. Martin, certain tax benefits had occurred in the past and a number of tax issues had to be considered. After corporate formality issues were addressed, it was decided with good tax advisors to keep The Spot in an S-Corp. and all liability arising from the restaurant and lounge would remain within the S-Corp, as long as the formalities were properly satisfied.

CASE STUDY: DAVID A TANZER

Ownership of the stocks would be transferred into the trust, which is permissible since it is a U.S. Domestic Grantor Trust for tax purposes allowing for ownership of S-Corp stock.

The Prof LLC was created for Dr. Martin's professional medical practice. To date she carried high professional liability coverage with expensive premiums. Even though she was only working part-time, she understood very well that she was at huge risk if an uncovered claim arose or liability occurred in excess of coverage — or worse yet, the insurance carrier went bankrupt. This separate LLC allowed better management of income and expenses for tax purposes. The result was ultimately lower taxes.

Arizona was selected as the choice for LLCs for U.S. based assets due to the Charging Order protection, and a Nevis or Cook Island's LLC for a future vacation home and investments.

Finally, an International Trust was created and registered in the Cook Islands. The Martins were both the Settlors and Protectors of the trust. If they died before the children reached 25 years of age, a successor Protector was named. Thereafter, when each child reached 25, they became Protectors of the trust. The trust would have the benefit of Charging Order protection by owning the LLCs as an added obstacle to persistent creditors.

What is the extent of the Martin's risk now? It is limited to less than 1 percent of the overall value of the assets. An impressive reduction in personal asset risk if they are personally sued.

The net value of the overall assets is approximately $4 million, plus $1 million term insurance for Mr. Martin and $500,000 term insurance for Dr. Martin. The Martin's 1 percent personal exposure to assets in the trust is less than $35,000 (remember, the home is 100 percent owned by the trust).

The estate tax savings for the Martins were substantial. Depending on asset valuations and gift giving to a Child's Trust, the present day estate tax savings was estimated somewhere between $1,000,000 and $2,000,000.

CASE STUDY: DAVID A TANZER

This was a substantial source of family wealth preservation for this estate, when viewed from the perspective that the Martins desired to pass their wealth to their children when they passed away, instead of putting it into government coffers. The cost for creating this tax savings is almost insignificant, comparatively speaking.

Liability insurance was still maintained on the nightclub, commercial real estate and the residential properties. And Dr. Martin still maintained professional liability coverage. However, with multiple levels of asset protection in place they were comfortable in reducing the limits of insurance coverage resulting in a substantial savings in annual insurance premiums. This alone was a significant cash flow benefit.

More details on the above and many other asset protection planning techniques are discussed in David Tanzer's book **How to Legally Protect Your Assets**, found at **www.DavidTanzer.com**

Briefly describe an unsuccessful story where assets were seized— this may well be the story of someone who came to you for advice after the lawsuit. Please change names as you think fit.

None of the clients that we have created International Trusts designed with integrated asset protection, whom have maintained the planning structure consistent with the provisions as established, have ever had any of their assets seized, or lost any of their assets.

A special feature of the LLC is that it can be set up with only one member, replacing a sole proprietorship formation. There is a tax advantage to this, but it may not present such a strong asset protection argument. If there is only one member, the LLC will be a disregarded entity for tax purposes and not just a pass-through entity. This means the LLC is treated as if it does not exist.

But there is no difference in state charging order laws between single- and multi-member LLCs. The charging order exists to avoid disruption to an operating business. If you recall, it was to stop the other business partners losing out just because one of the members has a liability that would otherwise take his share of capital away from the business. It is quite arguable that this is irrelevant if the LLC has a single member, so the asset protection possibilities are not quite so bulletproof.

The LLC, as you can see, is a strong business vehicle for tax minimization and asset protection. Though, you should not assume it is the best choice in all circumstances. There is no perfect choice, and you must weigh the pros and cons before committing to any particular form.

For example, because it is a comparatively recent entity, it has not been tested in every possible way in the courts. This means you may have an expensive fight against a challenge that has not come up and provided case law to rely on. Also, if you ever think you might go public, you cannot do so with the LLC — you need to use the C-Corporation. Consult with both your attorney and accountant before deciding.

As most states base their statutes for the formation of a LLC on the model Uniform Limited Liability Company Act (ULLCA) which was approved by the Commissioners on Uniform State Laws in 1996, there is a fairly consistent set of attributes that you will find. The ULLCA sets out the following characteristics:

- The LLC is a separate and distinct legal entity from its members.

- An LLC can have a fixed term or can exist in perpetuity.

- Managers and members of an LLC have limited liability — all they can lose is their investment.

- A member's interest can only be transferred with the consent of the other members.

- A member can transfer his interest in future distributions — but this does not transfer any membership rights.

- To dissolve an LLC, you need a fixed dissolution date, consent of the members, or dissolution by the state for non-compliance.

An important part of the formation of the LLC is the operating agreement. This is a document that sets out all the details of how distributions will be made and who gets which tax deductions, among other things. It needs to be drafted carefully, as it can have consequences in other ways. For instance, an operating agreement may spell out the services that each member will give to the company, which makes it an executory contract under the law. The advantage to this is that if a member suffers bankruptcy, the member's interest is better protected. As in many legal things, there is seldom a final answer to asset protection. Enough money can challenge any setup in court, so it is wise to take as much care as you can.

CHAPTER 8

Accounts Receivable

**"There's no business like show business, but there
are several businesses like accounting."
– David Letterman**

I f you are in business for yourself, it is possible that you have a lot of your money tied up in the business, in your equipment and inventory, and you have many customers with unpaid invoices. The idea of an accounts receivable program is to realize the funds from those unpaid invoices in advance so that the money can be put to some other use, and another benefit of the actions you take for this can be asset protection.

There are many businesses that sell goods and bill the customer, which inevitably means that their cash flow is lagging. This may mean that they have to take loans and pay interest on them so that they can pay their staff, even though the balance of their business income and expenditure would seem to be favorable. They may think that this is the nature of doing business, and some people accept this as inevitable.

Whatever other businesses do, you should know that accounts receivable programs or leveraged compensation programs are a great way to not only help your cash flow, but to provide solid asset protection, provided they are set up correctly. If you do not have a program, and your business has a debt liability, the creditor would be able to ask the judge to appoint a receiver, who can seize sufficient amounts of your accounts receivable to satisfy the judgment. Not only would you finish paying the full value demanded by the creditor, you may have cash flow problems for some time as part of the normal process of receiving money, which you then pay out to employees and suppliers would be interrupted.

THE ECONOMICS

While the details can become quite complex, the principles behind accounts receivable programs, also known as leveraged compensation programs, are easily understandable. If your business has unpaid invoices because your customers have not yet sent in their money, then you are able to implement this idea.

Your business can arrange a loan on the basis of your accounts receivable programs. The proceeds of this loan are then used in some way, typically to purchase a cash value annuity. As security for the loan, the lender has the accounts receivable and will usually place a National Uniform Commercial Code Form 1 (UCC1) lien on them. Frequently the lender will want to attach the cash value of the annuity as additional collateral.

The theory and advantage of doing this is that the loan proceeds will grow with compound interest and be tax deferred. The business will pay simple interest on the loan, assuming the amount of the loan remains stable. The power of compound interest will, over the course of some years, mean that you receive back in the annuity more than it has cost the business. On retirement, the sale of the business can pay back the principal borrowed against the accounts receivable, and the lender will release the annuity to fund their retirement.

In practice the benefits in cash terms may not be so clear. For instance, the growth rate on the annuity may not be sufficient to account for the interest payments, particularly if these are at a variable rate, so the plan may not actually generate additional value, but be a cost to the business. If the creditor forecloses on the accounts receivables, he would manage to secure any amount left over after the loan is paid back to the lender. Additionally, any action by the lender, if the business gets in trouble, would terminate the agreement and expose any excess amounts to creditors.

ASSET PROTECTION

Asset protection is one of the main reasons that you may want to continue considering an accounts receivable program. Your accounts receivable are an easy option for a creditor, as they can just take the checks as they come in from your customers. However, if you have set up your program correctly, the lender will have first call on the incoming funds, making them less of a target to the creditor. You should borrow sufficiently that there is no equity left in the accounts. The creditor may assume that the lender will foreclose on the accounts to satisfy the loan, and there will be nothing left for the creditor to take.

As has been said before, the more difficult you make it for the creditor to find and take your assets, the more likely he is to negotiate a reasonable settlement with you. Dealing with the assets in this way can never be considered a fraudulent transfer, as you have received fair value for them. It is possible for the creditor to foreclose on your accounts receivable even if there is no equity in them. This is unlikely because of the cost of foreclosure, but it would force your lender to terminate the loan and collect his money from your accounts receivable. As this would terminate the UCC1, any future receipts would be available to the creditor, so you could find yourself working purely for the benefit of the creditor until the judgment is paid. This illustrates why you should discuss all possibilities with your advisers to determine the best solution.

Now the obvious question is how to protect the value of the loan that you have received from seizure by a creditor. Frequently these funds are put towards an annuity or life insurance, because it is your insurance agent who will have suggested an accounts receivable program. This is with good reason though, as these products can feature tax-free or tax-deferred growth, and are typically protected by state law from creditors. You should know that there are other options, such as forming a LLC which receives the funds and invests them in other business ventures. The LLC enjoys charging order protection, which means that a creditor could not directly seize the capital. Before committing to any particular course, you must consider what most satisfies your needs and requirements.

RETIREMENT PLANNING

Retirement planning is the best known use of the accounts receivable programs that you will usually see. This is a good use of what some people think is an underused resource, the debt that your customers owe you. Really what you are doing is borrowing the money against your business, using it until you retire to make more money, then returning the original amount to your company. You need to work with your advisers to see if it is the best idea for you.

As stated above, you obtain a loan from your bank, paying interest to the bank each year. The money that you receive can be invested for compound growth with tax advantages through an insurance product, such as an annuity or life insurance, which is also protected from creditors. The loan is repaid when you sell your business or when you retire, either from the compounded account or from other assets, and the remainder will be available for your retirement. If your business expands in the years after setting up the accounts receivable program, you should review the amount and borrow more if necessary to take full advantage of the program and to restore full asset protection.

You should be wary of buying any pre-made solutions that are being sold by some insurance agents. You need to be aware of all the elements of the program you enter, and that they are in line with your goals. The plan needs to be worthwhile for your retirement as well as satisfying your asset protection requirements. You should examine the details, and only once you decide it is suitable go ahead and implement it.

Aspects that you will want to check with your advisers include how tax efficient the plan will be. You can do this by confirming the expected tax deductions. The extent of asset protection under your state's statutes should be another item on your checklist, for which you will need your advisers' help. Recognizing that your insurance agent may not be an expert in these other fields means that you will not be disappointed later by some unexpected revelations.

Part of your planning should include the method that you can use when you want to start taking in your retirement income. This will force you to look at your ideas for your business in the future. For instance, will you want it to be passed on to your family, or will you try to find a buyer? When the time comes that you want to retire, there will still be outstanding accounts receivable, and you may find that you can put these towards paying back the bank loan. If you sell the business, you could use some of the proceeds to pay off the loan. A third alternative is to give back the amount you borrowed from your investment vehicle.

LIFE INSURANCE

If you use the funds made available from your accounts receivable program to purchase life insurance, you will immediately have provided support for your family if you die prematurely. You will also be able to enjoy tax efficiency in many states. The lowest cost insurance, called term life insurance, only pays out on your death and does not have any intrinsic value, so it is not usually acceptable to your lender as collateral. While it is very useful for insurance purposes, it has no place in accounts receivable programs.

Other types of life insurance include whole life and universal life insurance. These policies build a cash value, in addition to providing a lump sum on death, and are suitable for use in this circumstance. Universal life is more flexible than whole life, and so is the preferred type of insurance.

Life insurance can be tax efficient. If you buy it personally, the premiums are not tax deductible, but if your employer buys it for the benefit of the employees, the employer can deduct the premiums as business expenses. The death benefits paid out are also usually exempt of taxes.

On the other hand, the asset protection properties vary from state to state. Many states exempt life insurance policies from the creditors grasp, but some do not. As you will see in the next chapter, there are ways to deal with this and provide asset protection. In summary, the accounts receivable finances will be paid to an irrevocable trust and the trust will buy the life insurance. Some experts recommend that you arrange your accounts receivable program in this manner, even if your state provides asset protection for life insurance, on the basis that the creditor may try to get around the statutes, and a trust provides further protection.

ANNUITIES

You may be familiar with the concept of annuities. They are built for retirement, which makes them a good fit for use with an accounts receivable program. They are a form of insurance to you, as for a payment now, or sometimes in installments, they will guarantee a certain income for as long as you live. The money will not run out regardless your age. This addresses a common worry of people reaching retirement, namely that their money may run out before they die.

As your actual lifespan may be very different from the average for your age group, this is an application which is sold by insurance companies who are used to taking such calculated risks. They have tables that tell them what average age you should live to, and work out the payments they can make for any amount invested accordingly.

You may like to think of it as the opposite of life insurance. With ordinary life insurance you pay regular amounts during your life, and the insurance company pays out a lump sum to your heirs on your death; with an annuity, you pay a lump sum and the company pays you regular amounts during your life.

In the accounts receivable application, you will purchase the annuity with one payment and receive the regular income at retirement. In other applications, you will find annuities that can be bought with a series of payments, and annuities that will start paying out as soon as you purchase them. Those are less in keeping with the intentions of the accounts receivable program. From a tax point of view, the funds that you pay into the annuity are returned to you without taxation; any earnings or growth will typically be taxed when it is paid to you.

You will also find that if you are comfortably off at retirement, you will be able to roll over the funds into another investment or annuity and defer taking money out. You need to choose what sort of investment vehicle the funds are put into, which will affect their growth. There may be a choice of a modest fixed guaranteed interest rate, or you can invest in a way which is more related to the performance of the stock market.

In practice, the fixed income annuity may not increase in value as much as is necessary to cover the costs of the loan. The loan will usually be a variable interest rate, and if this rises too high you will find that your accounts receivable program is costing you money. Of course, you will still have the asset protection feature, but you will be paying a premium for that.

On the other hand, the variable annuity which is linked to a stock market index may be subject to fluctuations, and your lender may also object to this, bearing in mind that he has the annuity value as backup collateral to your accounts receivable. This leaves us with the usual choice for accounts receivable program, which is called an equity indexed linked annuity.

The equity index annuity (EIA) is similar to a fixed annuity and will pay a certain basic interest rate. It is also linked to the performance of a market index, and if this is higher at the end of the term, then this will be the amount received. In this way, you have the safety of the fixed index, but with some measure of improved performance for the effects of inflation. The fixed rate of an EIA will often be less than that which you can receive with a fixed income annuity, as compensation for the linking component.

You will need a good adviser to help you select an EIA that suits you. There are a range of options to pick from for the market index which is followed, and because of the mechanics of investing, you will seldom find that the annuity will increase as much as the selected index. This must be, because of the minimum guaranteed fixed return even if the index sinks. A further point of note is that some EIAs have high early surrender charges, and if your lender closes your loan for any reason, you will be left having to pay these. The lender is almost certain to demand funds from your annuity rather than wait for the accounts receivable checks to trickle in. You will need to select your annuity carefully.

FACTORING

If asset protection by equity stripping is the goal, you may also consider accounts receivable factoring, also known as invoice financing. This is a well established practice and there are many companies, known as factors, in the business of factoring. The principle is that your accounts receivable are sold to the factor at a discounted price, and the factor is responsible for collections.

This has several advantages for the business owner. You don't have to wait to receive the majority of the money owed to you, and can put it to good use or secure it in an asset protected way. Having the factor following up on the invoices saves you time, and may mean that you do not need as much staff.

You will generally find that the factoring company will give you 70 to 90 percent of the face value of the invoices, depending how creditworthy your customers are. After the bills are paid, you will receive the rest of the money, less the fee charged by the factoring company, which can be as much as five percent.

Factoring is a tactic sometimes used by small companies when they are having cash flow problems and have no money on hand to pay their bills. Usually the factoring company will take a set of invoices to work on, so asset protection occurs in a piecemeal fashion. New accounts receivables would not be protected until they are submitted to the factor. In other ways the asset protection is good as the invoices are sold for fair value, and cannot constitute a fraudulent transfer.

In spite of the potential disadvantages of accounts receivable financing or leveraged compensation programs, there are a significant number of individual business owners who look to these programs as a way of protecting their assets.

There is no set formula for any business owner. Every business owner must carefully research each program presented and not simply take it at face value. Negotiating the terms of the accounts receivable financing program and getting information from other competing agents is necessary with any asset protection or financing program you set your mind to. It is also crucial to make sure the insurance agent or financial planner has experience and knowledge in the plan he sets before you. Anyone can sell a plan, but it takes someone knowledgeable to know how to administer it and bring forth yields that will benefit you financially.

As Ron Adkisson, author of *Financing Accounts Receivable for Retirement and Asset Protection*, said in a recent article on accounts receivable financing, "when accounts receivables plans work; it is a great vehicle for business owners to increase their retirement income as well as protecting a very vulnerable asset."

CHAPTER

9

Domestic Trusts

"It is impossible to go through life without trust: That is to be imprisoned in the worst cell of all, oneself."
– Graham Greene

Frequently, asset protection includes the use of some form of trust. Trusts are also used for tax reasons, and it is important that you are aware of the differences in treatment so that you can develop an idea of your best estate planning options. In this section, we will consider domestic trusts, which are defined as those trusts governed by the laws of one of the 50 states, and in the next section we will look at the possibility of using foreign trusts, which is sometimes a contentious topic.

Sometimes people get confused when they encounter trusts; it is true that there are many different types of trust, and it is easy to mix them up if you do not have them clearly understood in your mind. Possibly, corporations and companies are a more comfortable concept for some people, because they are more familiar territory. However, to consider only corporations and companies is to ignore a valuable side of the law that can be of benefit in many aspects of your life.

To start with the basics, you should understand that a trust is a simple concept. It is a development of the idea that you trust someone to take care of assets for the benefit of someone else. This means there are three parties in the formation of a trust. The first is called the settlor or grantor, and that is the person who initially has the assets and creates the trust. The settlor is responsible for the terms of the trust, and may or may not have future influence on the trust's operation once it is set up, depending on those terms.

The most important party to a trust is called the trustee, and he is the person who holds the assets, and distributes any income and the assets themselves as required by the terms of the trust. The trustee is legally obligated to take care of the assets as if they were his own, and has a duty to the beneficiary, but he cannot use the assets for his own benefit unless allowed by the trust. If he does not take care and operate the trust as required, then he can be sued by either of the other two parties.

The other person involved is called the beneficiary. He is the one who benefits from the trust, in accordance with the trustee's actions. That being said, he has nothing to do except wait for the trustee to implement the trust as required. In fact, the beneficiary has no control over the operation of the trust, unless the trustee is not acting in good faith.

For simplicity, I have described each party as a single person, but they can actually be any legal entity, for instance, it is common for a bank to be a trustee.

It is plainly obvious that the overall concept of a trust is simplicity itself. Every trust has the same basic structure, but the terms of the trust dictate how it is legally viewed for asset and taxation protection. One further item of note is that any party can be any person, and, for instance, one single person could be the settlor, trustee, and beneficiary, or any two of them. This has consequences for both asset protection and tax reasons, which will be explained later.

Most states do not require that the terms of a trust be set out in writing, but it would be unwise to proceed purely on oral agreement. The provisions of a trust can become very complex, so it is usual to have a written document prepared and signed. For asset protection purposes, this would be essential so the provisions could be tested in court and withstand scrutiny. The trust document may be referred to as the declaration of trust, or simply the trust. When a foreign trust is prepared, the document is often called a deed of settlement.

REVOCABLE TRUSTS

One of the most important things you should decide about a trust is whether it is a revocable or an irrevocable trust. As the name implies, you can change, or revoke, a revocable trust. Because of this, you will find that a revocable trust will not protect you from lawsuits.

Sometimes, it is not spelled out in the trust document whether it is revocable or not. This can be a grave error, as some states have laws that will decide which it is if not specified, and it may not be the one that you want. Your trust document should include specifying whether the settlor has the right to amend or alter the trust, or whether the settlor cannot ever affect the trust's operation.

It is easy to see why you achieve no asset protection by using a revocable trust. If the settlor can tear up the trust and take back the assets, then the court can direct him to do so if necessary to meet a creditor's claims. Having said that, there is a place in estate planning for the revocable living trust, which I will discuss below.

IRREVOCABLE TRUSTS

If you are looking to use a trust for asset protection it will inevitably need to be an irrevocable trust. The consequences of this are quite serious. It literally means that the settlor is unable to take back any assets should his circumstances change, or to make alterations in how the trust is operated.

While that is the legal position, you should note that a friendly trustee could be asked by the settlor to hand back the assets, and that they could voluntarily comply. There can be absolutely nothing in the trust document to ensure this, though.

For asset protection this must also be a funded trust, that is your assets must be placed into the trust, or they can be claimed by your creditors. This form of trust is called a living trust, as explained in the next section.

LIVING TRUST

You have probably heard of the living trust. For some years now it has been advocated as part of your estate planning, for reasons that will be explained. The living trust can also be called an inter vivos trust, this term being Latin for between the living. The other type of trust is called a testamentary trust, which is a trust that is created on the death of the settlor, as a result of his or her will.

When considered for estate planning, the living trust is usually revocable. It is intended to avoid the burden of probate. The trust can be created by one person, or by a married couple, and they control the assets within the trust. This is why it is not a good asset protection strategy.

When the settlor or settlors die, the trust continues and operates to distribute the assets as laid down in the declaration of trust. Because the assets are in the trust, they do not enter into the probate process. In fact, in a well-written trust there can also be a provision to save estate taxes, called an A-B provision, which ensures that the maximum estate tax exclusion is taken on the first death, and the separate assets put into a separate trust. If you are considering a living trust as part of your estate planning, you may wish to make sure that this item is included.

There is a trap in using a living trust for your estate planning. Several states have held that homesteading exemptions do not apply if the property is in a living trust, and you will need to be sure that this asset is protected in other ways.

However, it can be useful for tax purposes in circumstances such as the holding of assets in a family business. For example, a small developer building homes could title them in the Trust's name – this would not affect the sale to customers, but would protect them from being liable for estate tax on the untimely demise of the developer.

The homes could be owned by the family revocable trust, which would allow easy transfer of the remaining assets from the parents to the children when the parents were gone. This would legally avoid any probate taxes becoming due on the parents' death.

On the other hand, as the trust is revocable, it can just as easily be dissolved if it is no longer serving a valid purpose; an irrevocable trust, which would provide better asset protection, would not allow this flexibility.

TESTAMENTARY TRUST

As noted above, the alternative to a living, or inter vivos, trust is a testamentary trust. This trust is created by the settlor's will. Typically, this might be entertained by parents of small children who want to make sure the inheritance is held safely in trust until the children come of age.

Of course, as the testamentary trust only comes into being after death, it does not serve any purpose in avoiding probate. For the same reason, it also does not provide any asset protection for the settlor, although the trust may be written so that the beneficiaries' assets are protected. And finally, for obvious reasons, a testamentary trust must be irrevocable once it comes into being.

SELF-SETTLED TRUSTS

You may see the term self-settled trust used in some estate planning books. This is a trust where the settlor is also a named beneficiary. Even if the trust is set up as irrevocable, it is not likely that it will give much asset protection, even when the settlor is not also the trustee.

However, some states have enacted laws to permit self-settled trusts, and these are modeled after some foreign trusts, presumably to attract clients who would otherwise seek protection in that way. Alaska and Delaware passed the laws in 1997, and Nevada followed in 1999. Following that, Missouri, Oklahoma, Rhode Island, South Dakota, and Utah have also joined in. The fact that the statutes have not spread to other states indicates that these are not considered by many to be an effective tool.

The term domestic asset protection trust (DAPT) has been coined to describe these self-settled trusts. The idea is that they create a structure where the settlor creates a trust for his own benefit as beneficiary that also provides asset protection. As this runs counter to the normally accepted view on asset protection, and there is no definitive case law to sustain their legality, they should be viewed with caution at this time.

Apart from doubts about their efficacy in general, they can do nothing to protect assets from the federal government because of the Supremacy Clause, thus they are generally held to be inferior to the offshore protection schemes that are available.

DISCRETIONARY TRUSTS

We now consider a form of trust that is being used increasingly by the wealthy in their estate planning. This is called the discretionary trust, because the trust document gives discretion to the trustee on the disposition of the assets and income.

As with all effective asset protection trusts, the discretionary trust is irrevocable. This does not mean you cannot benefit from the assets. You can be a named beneficiary, and the trustee can distribute income or capital to you on a regular basis, in accordance with the terms of the trust. Those terms must not force the trustee to make the distribution; otherwise the asset protection is weakened.

The discretionary trust gives the trustee total discretion on which beneficiary to make payments to, and when to pay. It is preferable to have more than one beneficiary, as the terms of the trust can then allow the trustee to choose which beneficiaries benefit, and allow him to exclude one or more from the asset distribution.

Giving the trustee sole and absolute discretion over the distributions gives very good asset protection from a creditor. The fact is that a beneficiary cannot force the trustee to ever give him a distribution from the trust, and therefore a creditor, who cannot be in a stronger position, cannot force a payout either. Creditors have sought a provision in the proposed Uniform Trust Code that allows attachment of future distributions, but this still does not require that any distributions be made.

This relies on the trustee being friendly to the beneficiary, but this must be taken as a given with an irrevocable trust. If you were to become a mandatory beneficiary of the trust, the trust would be deemed a self settled trust and you would lose the protection in most states.

SPENDTHRIFT TRUSTS

The spendthrift trust is a basic trust form for asset protection. It is a provision in the trust that requires that the interest of a beneficiary may not be transferred, voluntarily or not, unless already allowed for by the terms of the trust document.

As long as the settlor is not also the beneficiary, this has historically been proven to provide almost complete asset protection. Most states prevent a self-settled spendthrift trust. The spendthrift clause would typically prevent anticipation or assignment of any interest in the asset, or any creditor's claim on the asset, before receipt by the beneficiary.

As long as it is not self settled, the reason that this is effective and allowed to stand court test is that no one has forced the settlor to set up the trust. The money is transferred into the trust on the settlor's terms, which preclude paying out in those ways that are prohibited by the terms.

A couple of points are worth noting: As this is a state provision, it would probably not stand against a federal claim. It would also not hold up if tested against child support or alimony. Some states limit their value against creditors who have provided necessities such as healthcare or food.

LIFE INSURANCE TRUSTS

Most people have life insurance, and it is often part of estate planning. Life insurance provides for survivors to ease the financial burden if the breadwinner dies, and can also be obtained in a business context to cover the loss of a key person. Life insurance is usually not included in probate, as the proceeds are paid to a named beneficiary and are never part of the estate. This does not mean that the IRS will not include its value when calculating your estate tax, and frequently it is the life insurance that increases the estate's value so that tax is due.

You need to be aware that there are three parties to every life insurance policy. One is the policy owner, another is the insured person, and the beneficiary is the last. Many people only think of these last two when considering insurance, and with good reason; the owner is usually the same person as the insured. You are permitted to own a life insurance policy on the life of someone else, although they have to be someone in whom you have an insurable interest — either a family member or a business colleague, not just a random person.

As the owner, you are responsible for paying the premiums. You can also decide to cancel the insurance, if you want, and change who the beneficiary is. It is important that the owner can be a separate entity to the insured and the beneficiary for asset protection purposes.

There are two types of life insurance, which is also relevant to what the assets are that you are protecting. Straight insurance on a life, which pays out the agreed amount on death but has no other value, is called term life. This is the cheapest type of insurance, and as there is no value on it until your death this may or may not be something that your creditors would look at.

The other type of insurance, which is preferred by insurance agents as it has the potential for higher commissions, is called whole life insurance, and this includes an element of investment in your substantially higher premium. These policies are available with various mixes and proportions of investment, but are all based on the same idea. There is a surrender value associated with these policies, which is small for the first few years, but increases later. If you are the owner, this would certainly be an asset that your creditors could try to attach.

Even if you have a whole life policy, there are several states that have laws to provide an exemption, which may be either the death benefit or the surrender value. Some states exempt only a portion of the surrender value. It is quite common for the beneficiary of the death benefit to be shielded, although only if the beneficiary is a dependent. It is necessary to find out what the current laws are in your state so you can determine how much is safe from creditors.

There is a means to shield your life insurance from creditors and to avoid it being included in the estate for calculation of estate taxes, and that is by using a life insurance trust. This is known as an irrevocable life insurance trust (ILIT) and is a trust specifically designed to hold a life insurance policy. As it is irrevocable, you cannot get at the assets and they are therefore not available to your creditors. If structured correctly, the benefit on death is not included in the estate, which allows the funds to be used in the way that you probably had in mind when taking out the insurance, that of helping your survivors financially.

It is commonly known that the proceeds from a life insurance policy are not subject to income tax. What most insurance agents do not tell you is that the death benefit is included by the IRS in your estate, no matter who the beneficiary is. The solution to this is, as you may have realized, using an ILIT, which will own the insurance policy. As you no longer own the policy, it does not come into your estate for tax purposes. The trust would be the beneficiary, and not your estate.

Regarding the mechanics of the insurance, usually you would have to pay monthly or annual premiums to keep it in force. You should note that the premiums have to be paid by the trust, and not by you; otherwise you will lose the asset protection and tax benefit. You therefore must pay the trustee, who is responsible for keeping up the insurance payments. The alternative is to fully fund the insurance in advance, making it a fully paid policy, which you would transfer ownership of to the trust.

It seems that this sort of irrevocable trust would be a simple answer for other assets, and certainly trusts can form a part of your estate planning. The reason you cannot just adopt this technique with all your assets to avoid inheritance tax and seizure by creditors is the IRS has an interest in transferring assets, otherwise known as a gift tax. If you were to transfer your assets to an irrevocable trust, you would have made a gift to the trust, and would owe gift tax. It is not generally thought a good idea to pay a tax now to avoid a tax in the future, particularly if there are other potential ways to avoid the future tax.

The way this works for life insurance is that the gift is not counted as being worth the death benefit, but only the surrender value, or roughly equivalent to the annual premium for a term policy. That means life insurance is the one asset that can be picked out in this manner, with no further complication.

There is still one more problem with this — you do not want to pay any gift tax. You may know that you can make a gift of up to $12,000 to any person each year, and it is exempt from the gift tax. However, strictly speaking, this is for a present gift, and a gift to a trust does not qualify as a present gift. So, you would be taxed for all the funds that you pay to the trust for the premiums, as well as the value when the insurance was initially transferred.

The answer to this was found and proved in court in 1968 by Clifford Crummey. He argued that if you write the trust so that the beneficiaries of the trust have the right to withdraw money from the trust in the same year you give money to it, then it qualifies as a present interest, and will be tax-free, at least up to the $12,000 annual exemption. Note that the beneficiaries do not have to withdraw money, and indeed you do not want them to, as the funds are for the insurance premium — to cover the legalities, each year they should be offered the funds in writing, in what has become known as a Crummey letter, to which they would respond that they do not wish to withdraw any money.

There are two more points to note about an ILIT before moving on. It is actually a more flexible instrument than a straight insurance contract, as the trust can be directed in the manner that the funds will be distributed, rather than just naming a beneficiary, as in a normal policy. For instance, you can direct that the funds are paid to the beneficiaries over a period of years rather than at one time, and the trustee will comply. On the other hand, you might direct that the estate taxes and costs are paid out of the death benefit first, and the remainder distributed to the beneficiaries.

Finally, on a point of law, the tax code directs that if you die within three years of setting up the ILIT, the value of death benefit will be included in your estate for tax purposes. The sooner you take action on your estate plan, the less likely your heirs are to run into this problem.

CHILDREN'S TRUSTS

As with the ILIT, we are now considering trusts established for specific purposes or assets. The irrevocability principle for asset protection applies to any established for this purpose. If the trust is revocable, then you as settlor still have a means to access the funds, and that means your creditors can make you do so.

An irrevocable children's trust (ICT) gives you asset protection, and can also have tax benefits. If you transfer assets to this type of trust they are protected from your creditors and they are no longer part of your taxable estate. Any income generated by the assets would be taxed at a lower tax rate, as it would count as your children's.

The terms of the trust, which is in accordance with Section 2503 Minor's Trust, ensure that the assets are not touchable by you or your creditors, and by the child beneficiary while under the age of 21. The only drawback to this arrangement is that the funds are available to the child when they are 21, which you may still consider too young for responsible behavior, depending on the child. As it is irrevocable, you as settlor or grantor can have no further say in the disposition of the assets, and can only ask the 21-year-old for his or her consent to leave the assets in trust.

CHARITABLE REMAINDER TRUSTS

Funding a charitable remainder trust (CRT) may seem to be a strange way to protect your assets, as you will be giving away your assets to protect them. However, there are some ways in which this technique can benefit both you and the charity financially, and they are worth considering if you have a philanthropic desire.

The classic way in which this provides you with a benefit is if you own assets that have appreciated in value that you can donate to the charity, and can obtain a regular income from those assets during your lifetime. The charitable remainder trust benefits the charity, gives you a tax deduction in the year you set it up, and gives you an income for life.

Consider, for instance, that you may own some shares that you bought for $40,000, and they are now worth $100,000. If you sold them you would become liable for capital gains taxes, currently $9,000 on the $60,000 gain. On your death, if your estate is large enough and would be liable for estate taxes there would be a tax deduction of $40,000, leaving $60,000 for your heirs.

Alternatively, you could transfer your shares to a CRT, with yourself named as the income beneficiary for the remainder of your life. This would give you a tax deduction for the $100,000 charitable contribution, and avoid any capital gains. With the tax deduction you could afford to buy an insurance policy that could replace the $60,000 that your heirs were hoping for on your death, and you would not have to pay any capital gains at any time. You would continue to get the income during your lifetime, and the shares would be fully protected from any creditors. When you die, the charity receives the full value of your gift, including income.

QUALIFIED PERSONAL RESIDENCE TRUST

One of the less well-known trusts is the qualified personal residence trust (QPRT), which is specially set up for your personal residence. As there are other ways to protect your residence that allow you to take advantage of the capital gains exemptions should you move, the QPRT may not suit your circumstances.

If you wanted to use a QPRT, you would transfer your house to the trust, and the trust terms would include your tenancy in the house for a set time, usually ten years. At the end of this term, the trust transfers the property to your beneficiaries. The idea behind this is that the house is transferred at a lower value than otherwise, which would reduce the estate taxes due on your death.

This technique protects your home from creditors, as the only claim they can have is for the right to use the home for ten years, or the remaining period. The house itself is owned by the trust, and thus safe from seizure. It does not necessarily protect the house from your beneficiaries' creditors; you would have to ensure a spendthrift clause was included to prevent transfer of the property to others rather than the beneficiary.

QUALIFIED TERMINABLE INTEREST PROPERTY TRUSTS

The Qualified Terminable Interest Property Trust is also a less well-known type of trust, and can be valuable in certain specific circumstances. This type of trust is most suitable for people who have been married before, who want to ensure that their children from a previous marriage are taken care of, in addition to their current spouse. It is not actually used for asset protection, apart from sheltering your assets from your spouse to the extent that you ensure they will be available later for the children.

The qualified terminable interest property trust (QTIP) gives your surviving spouse a lifetime income from the trust, and then the principal passes to your children upon your spouse's death. It is a testamentary trust, so provides no asset protection during your lifetime. When it is formed on your death, it then shields the assets from any of your spouse's creditors, and avoids estate tax until your spouse dies.

LAND TRUST

This type of trust has been heavily advertised by some advisers, who claim that it can hide the property owner's identity, provide full asset protection, save taxes, and even avoid due-on-sale clauses in house finance. The truth is, there is some protection from using a properly drafted land trust, and the protections are best in Illinois and Florida, as they have been tested through case law, although there are a few other states with land trust provisions.

The trustee of a land trust is frequently a bank, and the real estate is titled to the trustee, so at first sight there is some hiding of the ownership. You would be the beneficiary of the trust, and there is no need to divulge the beneficiary of a trust. However, some states require full disclosure of the beneficiaries where the transfer of title of real property is involved. Arizona, for example, has such a law. There would also be a public record of how the land came into the trust's ownership, and that is likely to allow the true ownership to be determined.

Regarding asset protection, this is by no means as secure as has been touted. As you have a beneficial interest in a land trust, your creditors may be successful in applying to seize that interest, which means the best you can hope for is that the path to track down your assets is not followed too closely by the attorneys. The truth is, the trust is revocable, and you are the grantor and beneficiary, so there is no relinquishing of control of the property, and your creditors can access it. Even if the trust is set up to be irrevocable, this merely entails more paperwork and taxes, and you would still be both grantor and beneficiary, making it a self-settled trust that is vulnerable to your creditors.

The tax savings that are thought to attach to a land trust are not realistic. For instance, some people think the IRS will not be able to find out who the real owner is, saving income taxes. The IRS reports on its Web site that it is watching out for such abuses.

Finally, it is doubtful if it is legal to suggest that the trust can be changed to benefit someone else, effectively selling the property for consideration, without triggering the due-on-sale provision of the loan. Certainly if the mortgage company found out that you had sold your interest in the property by this means they would regard it as a change of ownership. In addition, if you want to do a 1031 exchange of rental property, you will need to transfer the property from the trust.

If there is any point in a land trust, it may be in avoiding probate. A living trust can cover this and other assets though, so there is no advantage having a separate trust for this purpose. Also, there is some ownership privacy afforded if you happen to live in one of the few states that have implemented separate statutes for a land trust.

MEDICAID TRUST

The Medicaid trust is the last special trust structure that we will consider here. It is irrevocable, and can give asset protection. The primary purpose of the Medicaid trust is to reduce your assets to the level that you can qualify for Medicaid to pay nursing home costs.

As the settlor, you transfer your assets to the trust, and can be an income beneficiary of the trust. Your children are the residual beneficiaries, receiving the assets after death. The trust is under direction to pay you income up to the maximum amount allowed under Medicaid, and, without ownership of your assets, you can qualify for Medicaid nursing home assistance. The chief problem with a Medicaid trust is that you must create it and fund it at least five years before applying for Medicaid, and it is difficult to anticipate that far in advance whether you will need it. If you do not need it, you have tied up your assets in an irrevocable trust, and thus lose access to and control of them.

10 Foreign Trusts

"Do not trust all men, but trust men of worth; the former course is silly, the latter a mark of prudence."
- Democritus

Foreign trusts, and other offshore accounts, have been widely regarded as the ultimate asset and tax protection tool, even if rather exotic and probably only for the rich and famous. Opinions vary on the veracity of this view, which may be more rooted in the perceptions of a decade ago than in current conditions. On the one hand, you have advisers who say that a properly structured estate, including offshore provisions, is the ultimate planning arrangement; on the other hand, some advisors have seen too many people deluded by seminars that promised ultimate protection to those who signed up for an offshore trust which was not in their best interest. In this chapter, we will examine the realities as they exist today.

Whatever asset protection and tax saving strategies you implement in your personal financial and estate plan you need to make sure that your legal advisers are experienced in the particular field, and that the plan is prepared with a view on all conceivable contingencies. This is the overriding lesson that major consultants in the field repeat in all their advice, and it is especially applicable when you are dealing with offshore matters, where you may not feel that you have familiarity or control.

ADVANTAGES

One of the vigorous proponents of offshore planning is Arnold S. Goldstein, Ph.D., author of *So Sue Me!*, who avers that "your money is never safer than when it's outside the country and beyond the reach of the American courts." Examine what advantages you can have with a properly drafted and executed plan including offshore elements.

The main advantage of offshore investments is that they are not governed by U.S. laws, but by the laws of the country. This is helpful in several ways. First, the U.S. courts do not have jurisdiction over them, and cannot force accounts to be returned to the United States, unless there is an inter-country agreement. We will look at which countries have the most favorable laws for this purpose. This does not mean that the court cannot order you to return the funds, and if you have that control over them you would be in serious trouble should you not exercise that power. That is why foreign irrevocable trusts can form a basis for your plan, in that you turn over control of the assets to a trustee, and do not have the legal authority to demand their return.

Other countries have their own laws, and unless they are anarchic, court cases can be established under the country's own laws. In the best of countries, these laws are not as favorable to creditors as they are in the United States, and the additional complication and expense of new litigation may also make your creditors hesitate to follow the money. Part of asset protection is to make it economically difficult to seize the assets, so that the claimant decides that the task is not worth undertaking.

A previous chapter discussed how an asset transfer could be found to be a fraudulent conveyance, even if there was no knowledge of a lawsuit at the time. If the transfer is found to be fraudulent, and the assets are in the jurisdiction of the United States courts, then it is a simple paper exercise for the transfer to be voided and the assets seized. This is not the case if the assets are in a different country's jurisdiction, and thus there is some protection against predated claims.

In fact, in many countries there is a statute of limitations that requires the timely filing of a lawsuit for it to be considered, and this may invalidate some claims, particularly as it takes some effort to re-submit a case in a foreign country and under different laws. Another obstacle is that in many places the creditor must prove beyond a reasonable doubt that the transfer of funds was fraudulent, which is a very different criteria from that exercised in the United States. Often laws in other countries tend to be more in favor of the debtor than the creditor, particularly if that country has sought to make itself attractive for foreign investment.

If you have assets abroad, you have a wide range of investments available to you, much wider than you can find in the United States alone, so your assets can grow at a faster pace. The United States Securities and Exchange Commission makes it difficult for foreign companies to sell their stock in this country; so foreign assets open up this marketplace for the investor. Particularly relevant at the current time is your diversification away from the dollar, which seems to be depreciating at an alarming rate. As you can hold your assets in other currencies, you will be less exposed to currency fluctuations.

One sometimes intimated advantage is tax savings. Unfortunately, this is often in the context of hiding your assets from the IRS so you do not pay income or capital gains taxes on them; this is against the law. This counts as tax evasion, which is illegal, and you should know that the IRS is actively pursuing people who behave in this manner. However, tax planning should be a part of your offshore portfolio, which will at least be tax neutral. To repeat, Americans are liable for income tax on all their income, no matter where in the world it is earned, and to try to hide this away is a serious offense. You achieve better financial privacy by using offshore accounts, and you must follow the required tax reporting rules in order to continue enjoying this.

The statistics support the favorability of transferring assets abroad for protection. Fewer than 3 percent of judgment creditors even attempt to satisfy their judgments with offshore assets, and even among those the case is often settled for a fraction of the claim.

DISADVANTAGES

Overseas trusts have been oversold, that is a demonstrable fact. Investors have been tempted with the promise of ironclad asset protection and, perhaps, the thought of saving income tax by some less-than-honest dealing. Add to this the idea that a visit to another country could be claimed as a tax deduction if your accounts are held there, and it is easy to see why many people fell for the pitch. An advocate for the point of view that offshore planning may not be worth the cost is Mark J. Kohler, attorney and CPA, who in his book, *Lawyers are Liars,* says, "for the average American, I believe off shore should be off limits." He does not dismiss it entirely, but emphasizes that the cost and the need to make sure it is done correctly, if at all, have to be balanced against the potential gains. One of his main complaints is that some promoters try to offer a standard solution for everyone, and that each plan should be individually tailored for the particular situation.

For the offshore planning to be successful, it is not sufficient that the account is located elsewhere. You must also give up any semblance of control over the assets, which is a factor that you need to take into your assessment of the viability. If you have any ability to force the assets to be repatriated in satisfaction of a judgment, you must exercise it or face jail time for contempt.

This fact was forcibly demonstrated by two court cases around the turn of the century. The Federal Trade Commission brought a case against Affordable Media, LLC, in 1998, which was decided in favor of the FTC in 1999. Denyse and Michael Anderson who ran Affordable Media sold investment interests in their company, which was run as a Ponzi scheme. This means that later investments were used to pay dividends for the early investors, and true cash flow was not being generated as promised. They had created a trust in the Cook Islands, which is one of the countries favored for offshore trusts.

The Andersons were co-trustees and trust protectors, which are explained later. When they were ordered by the court to repatriate the funds, they were terminated by the Cook Island trustee, as required by an antiduress provision, resigned as trust protectors, and claimed that they could not access the funds. The U.S. court determined that this was a false claim, as they had control of the trust. There was a similar outcome in the case of Goldberg v. Lawrence, which was decided in 2000. Vernon Jacobs is familiar with the issues of this case, and why it failed. He has particular expertise in foreign matters and tax compliance.

CASE STUDY: VERNON JACOBS

Vernon Jacobs is a CPA and CLU who provides tax compliance services to U.S. persons that own a foreign corporation, foreign partnership, foreign trust, or various foreign investments. He is a prolific author and the President of Offshore Press, Inc., a family owned company that publishes his books and newsletters. (**www.offshorepress.com**)

In what way are you involved with asset protection, and does this include general estate planning, such as for tax issues?

I'm the author of a twice monthly e-mail newsletter and subscription Web site that provides extensive information about asset protection and related tax issues. I believe that providing asset protection services is "the practice of law" and that those who provide such services without having a law degree and a license to practice law are subjecting themselves to serious malpractice problems and their own malpractice coverage will not provide redress to their clients.

CASE STUDY: VERNON JACOBS

Do you specialize in any particular aspects of asset protection, such as foreign trusts or LLCs?

My focus is on the tax treatment of foreign asset protection methods but is not limited to the use of foreign entities.

In your experience, do you find that a single entity or strategy is sufficient for most people, or do you commonly recommend a multi-layered structure?

The complexity of an asset protection plan should be based on the size of the client's estate, his or her risk exposure and his or her tolerance for dealing with the complexities of multi-layered structures. Multiple entities that are properly structured can provide greater asset protection, but the added protection might not justify the added cost of establishing the multiple entities and maintaining them over an extended time.

Have you found that you have needed to change your methods in recent years, because of FTC v. Affordable Media, or to include Nevis LLCs?

The Anderson case and a number of similar cases involved foreign trusts which the U.S. courts believed were not truly independent of the trust grantor. A foreign trust can be an effective method of asset protection if the grantor is willing to transfer genuine control to the foreign trustee and if the grantor can demonstrate that the funds in the foreign trust are not necessary to maintain his or her lifestyle. The Nevis LLC is reputed to have the best statute in the world for protecting the assets inside the LLC, even if it is a single member LLC. That should be the recommended method when the client is unwilling or unable to relinquish complete control over the assets in a foreign trust.

However, there is concern among many U.S. lawyers that a single member LLC may be disregarded by the U.S. courts and that if the member has the power to recover assets from the LLC, a U.S. judge will simply order him or her to transfer funds from the LLC to a creditor. But I'm not aware of any cases where this has happened.

CASE STUDY: VERNON JACOBS

Briefly describe a "success" story, that is, an asset protection plan that was threatened in some way and withstood the attack, and why. Please change names as you think fit.

To a large extent, the Anderson case was successful until the Andersons got tired of sitting in a jail cell. The Trustee (whom I know) refused to relinquish the assets as long as the Andersons were under court duress. Most of the real success stories involve people who have been sued, lost and had a judgment issued against them, but were able to negotiate a very substantial discount on the amount of the judgment. And, perhaps the most successful stories are those where a judgment creditor simply gives up and doesn't even attempt to collect when assets are held in a foreign trust.

Briefly describe an unsuccessful story where assets were seized — this may well be the story of someone who came to you for advice after the lawsuit. Please change names as you think fit.

I haven't provided asset formation services to any clients and therefore have not had that kind of experience.

But, I do know of three cases where a U.S. person entered into a private annuity contract with a U.S. promoter who was collaborating with the owner of a foreign corporation. The U.S. people entered into an agreement to sell a valuable asset (stock in a successful business) to the foreign buyer in exchange for a life income annuity where the payments were deferred until the retirement age of the U.S. person. In each case, the foreign buyer made endless excuses about not being able to make the payments when they became due. In all three cases, I was contacted to help the U.S. seller to recover his assets or to force the foreign buyer to comply with the contract. In each case, I referred the person to an attorney but the attorney was not able to secure any performance from the foreign buyer. In one case I ended up making a referral to a second lawyer who was able to secure a partial recovery.

CASE STUDY: VERNON JACOBS

If relevant, what changes did you recommend to improve the asset protection in this last case?

I inform people that they are subject to the honesty of the foreign buyer of their property and to the laws in a foreign jurisdiction and to the assistance of the judiciary in a foreign country.

However, because I am a tax accountant, I am most often asked for tax advice about various offshore arrangements and I have been able to offer suggestions as to alternative tax arrangements. The U.S. tax laws involving foreign trusts, LLCs, and foreign corporations are very complex and are very different from the laws that apply to domestic entities of the same kind. Non-compliance penalties are far more severe and the U.S. government is presently engaged in a virtual witch-hunt to locate every kind of non-compliance with respect to the disclosure of foreign investments and transactions.

As mentioned in the previous section, the implication that the funds are somehow beyond the IRS because they are in a different jurisdiction, and thus capable of being tax-sheltered, is erroneous. In addition to having to satisfy the taxation requirements of the United States, there is an additional onerous reporting requirement that is required by the IRS. The fine for not complying with this reporting of certain transactions is appreciable, at $100,000, and this requirement is too often overlooked when the apparent advantages of offshore planning are mentioned.

TRUST PROVISIONS

Consider how it is intended to work: a foreign trust is similar in formation to a domestic trust. There is the settlor, or grantor, the trustee, and the beneficiary. A fourth party, the trust protector is a kind of trust overseer, and his powers are covered later, although often it is better not to have one appointed.

If the settlor has a judgment against him, the ideal would be for him to be able to say that he does not have the assets, and that he has no way of obtaining the assets. The assets are owned by the overseas trust. The court in the United States has no jurisdiction over the foreign trust, and cannot order the trustee to repatriate the assets. Indeed, the foreign trustee has a duty to the beneficiaries to not allow the assets to pass to a creditor, as they could be sued in the foreign country by the beneficiaries for doing this, and could even lose their license to act as a trust company.

In a similar way to the domestic trust, it is important that the provisions of the foreign trust are set out in writing. However, it does not have to be in a foreign language, and does not need to be signed in a foreign country. The essence of it is that it spells out, in detail, that the trust is governed in all respects by the laws of that country, and is exclusively answerable to the courts in that country, and no other. There will be an agency in the country where the trust will need to be registered, similar to the Registrar of Trusts.

Typically, a foreign trust needs to be irrevocable if it is for asset protection purposes. This is for similar reasons to the domestic trust, for if it was revocable, a judge could order the settlor to revoke it and make the assets available for creditors. If the settlor refused, he could be held in contempt, as he is fully under the laws of the United States.

In addition, the foreign trust should be discretionary, so that the trustee never has to make a distribution to a beneficiary. The trust should be written so the trustee can decide to withhold distributions for any reason that he considers advisable, which would include the circumstances that the trustee knew that the funds would be forfeited to a creditor.

One of the features included in many foreign trusts is an antiduress clause, as mentioned above. This requires the trustee to only recognize instructions or advice when he knows that it is given by people of their own free will and to ignore anything that he thinks comes out of duress, including court directives. This is an essential element, as it allows the settlor to comply with a U.S. court's directive to try and obtain the assets without actually exposing them. The request is made, so that the settlor cannot be held in contempt of the court, but the trustee has been previously instructed and thus is bound to ignore it by reason of the duress. The trustee has no relationship to the U.S. legal system, and thus cannot be summoned or held in contempt for this action, or lack of action.

SELF-SETTLED TRUSTS

The concept of a self-settled trust is discussed in the domestic trust chapter. The self-settled trust has the settlor the same person as the beneficiary, and it provides no protection of the assets in the domestic environment, with the exception of some states that have passed specific laws modeled on the foreign trust.

While it is true that a foreign trust can be a self-settled trust, it is not recommended that the settlor is the sole beneficiary. If other beneficiaries are named, such as spouse or children, then the trustee has discretion to make distributions to these others if the settlor is under a judgment. This makes sure the assets are not required to be distributed at any time to the benefit of the creditors.

THE TRUST PROTECTOR

Many of the countries that are used for foreign trusts have their laws based in English law, and this is the reason that there can be a fourth party to the trust, called a trust protector. The trust protector sits in an overseeing position over the settlor, trustee, and beneficiaries, and is allowed to step in if he sees something going wrong with the trust's operation. In fact, there is usually a provision that he can dismiss the trustee and appoint another if there is a reason to do so.

Other powers of the trust protector can include cutting out beneficiaries, moving the trust to another jurisdiction, and other management functions. You can see that with these powers, you have control over the assets, regardless of any other trust provisions, thus it is unwise for the settlor to also be the trust protector, as this would negate any asset protection. This was the principal problem with the Anderson's case. They could not resign and then claim that they could not satisfy the judgment of the court, as it was totally within their ability to retrieve the assets as ordered by the court. In fact, if the only choice for a trust protector would be a U.S. citizen, it is better that you do not have one, as otherwise the trust protector would be subject to the court's orders, and would have to exercise their powers to the great detriment of the protection that you are seeking.

CHOICE OF TRUSTEE

The role of the trustee, as you can see, is a vital one in ensuring that the trust operates as intended, particularly when threatened by lawsuits. The countries that typically are used for foreign trusts have extensively catered for the business that they are attracting, and you should find no shortage of possible candidates. The trust company must be registered and licensed as such, but this in itself does not ensure that they will work in the way that you wish. The best answer is to find a trust company by personal recommendation. You can ask your U.S. estate advisers, if they have experience of foreign trust companies, or at least you should ask prospective companies for references who you can talk to.

One question you may come across is whether you should be a co-trustee of your own foreign trust. At one time it was thought that this would work well, as having an American based trustee allowed easy access to the assets when needed, without having to send documents abroad for signature. The asset protection side would be covered by the co-trustee resigning if there was a problem looming with creditors. This was one of the factors considered in the case of the Andersons, so now the advice is usually to avoid doing it.

Another question is whether the trustee company should have an office in the United States. Again, this would provide greater convenience for operating the trust. It is true that the general operation of the trust would be made easier if there was a local office; if you have asset protection as one of your goals, though, it would be most unwise to have an American agent. Such an office could be subjected to American court orders, and held in contempt of the court if they did not comply. In effect, this would be no better than a domestic trust.

CHOICE OF COUNTRY

There are a number of countries that want to have your business, and have enacted laws that are favorable for foreign trust. Some have been around for a time, and others appear at intervals seeking to get into the market. I would advise you to stick with the countries that have a long history of accommodating trusts. If your financial adviser in this country has particular experience with a trust company, then, provided it meets all the criteria, you should consider their recommendation.

In a short list of countries to consider, the Cook Islands, Nevis, Gibraltar, Belize, Turks & Caicos, Saint Vincent, and the Grenadines are all included. Of these, Nevis has become popular recently, particularly as they also have an LLC regulation that is proving to be effective, and this is discussed later in the chapter. You should have regard to the following criteria in the selection of a country for your foreign trust.

Determine how long their statute of limitation is. The shorter time the better, as it allows less time for your creditor to organize a case to challenge a fraudulent transfer. Nevis has the shortest time, at one year.

You want to choose a country that does not recognize foreign judgments. For instance, there are treaties between many major countries that require reciprocal recognition of the judgments of the other country. This applies, for instance, between the United States and England. The treaty requires England to recognize the judgments of the United States, and for the United States to recognize English court judgments. Even if there is no formal treaty, some countries will still give some weight to a judgment under the doctrine of comity, which basically covers an understanding that the legal system makes fair decisions. These criteria rule out many foreign countries.

Having covered that issue, it is necessary that the law of the country is not disregarded by the United States as being invalid. As an example, if the United States does not accept that your foreign trust is indeed a trust, you may find that you have taxation problems.

Another factor that can arise with some countries is whether they will tax the trust's assets or any earnings arising out of the assets. You will have to pay United States taxes where applicable, and you do not want to find that your property is subject to such controls in the country that you form your trust in.

Other factors include exchange controls that may inhibit you enjoying your funds as you intend, amount of privacy that you can expect, and whether they truly have self-settled trust and the higher standard of proof for fraudulent transfers, as mentioned above. All the countries I have named include these essentials.

Patricia Donlevy-Rosen specializes in asset planning issues, and finds that frequently offshore trusts are part of the best solution.

CASE STUDY: PATRICIA DONLEVY-ROSEN

Patricia Donlevy-Rosen, President and a Shareholder of Donlevy-Rosen & Rosen, P.A., **www.ProtectY-ou.com**, is an AV-rated Attorney practicing in Miami, and is also admitted to practice law in New York. Her firm represents clients throughout the United States in asset protection planning. Ms. Donlevy-Rosen is a frequent lecturer and author on asset protection planning and corporate and business planning subjects.

Ms. Donlevy-Rosen is the author of **Asset Protection Planning, a Tax Advisors Planning Series** book, published by Research Institute of America, and used by attorneys, CPAs, and estate planners researching asset protection planning issues. She is also the co-editor and publisher of **The Asset Protection News** and has published numerous articles in professional and academic journals. Ms. Donlevy-Rosen is a member of the Board of Advisors of the Southpac Offshore Planning Institute (SOPI), the Asset Protection Planning Committee of the Real Property, Probate and Trust Law Section and the International Law Section of the ABA, the Business Law and the Real Property, Probate and Trust Law Sections of the Florida Bar. Ms. Donlevy-Rosen has a Juris Doctor degree from New York Law School (Cum Laude) where she was Notes and Comments Editor of the Law Forum and a member of the Student Bar Association. She has a Bachelor of Arts Degree (in Economics) from Vassar College.

She can be reached at PDR09@ProtectYou.com, or at (305) 447-0061, Ext. 3.

CASE STUDY: PATRICIA DONLEVY-ROSEN

In what way are you involved with asset protection, and does this include general estate planning, such as for tax issues?

My firm focuses on estate and business planning that always includes asset protection planning with offshore trusts.

Offshore trusts are not necessarily foreign trusts (foreign trust is a tax term, and when a trust becomes a foreign trust different tax reporting comes into play). Where the facts indicate, a client's structure may include one or more LLCs. If the need for an LLC is to hold liquid assets, the LLC may well be formed offshore. If the need for an LLC is to hold U.S. real estate, then the LLC will be formed in the state where the real estate is located. Our planning incorporates all the gift and estate tax planning that is involved in conventional estate planning.

Do you specialize in any particular aspects of asset protection, such as foreign trusts or LLCs?

We use offshore trusts as the core of our asset protection structures. (Note, offshore trusts are not always foreign trusts. The term foreign trust is a tax term, the term offshore trust is a term of art that means a trust where at least one trustee is domiciled in a foreign jurisdiction, and the laws of a foreign jurisdiction govern the administration of said trust.) While structures set up by my firm nearly always use an offshore trust, my portion of our practice focuses on the protection of assets that cannot be physically moved into a trust. Despite the change of title on property, if the property remains in the U.S. changes or transfers in title can be undone based on fraudulent transfer or conveyance rules or other reasons. Instead, I represent our clients in removing the value or equity from their immovable/fixed/real property assets.

People are often under the impression that transferring title of their assets to a trust (domestic or offshore) will protect assets from claims. This may be true if: (a) title has been in the trust for a period longer than the applicable fraudulent transfer or fraudulent conveyance statute, (b) the settlor is not in bankruptcy,

CASE STUDY: PATRICIA DONLEVY-ROSEN

as there is now a ten year look back in bankruptcy for transfers to a trust, and (c) a U.S. court respects the transfer. With respect to an offshore trust this will be true if the asset itself can be moved by the trustee offshore before or at the critical time (when faced with a serious threat from a third party), so that no U.S. court will have jurisdiction over it.

However, assets such as equipment, real estate (including a home or office building), and accounts receivable (immovable assets) cannot be moved offshore. Therefore, if an individual were to title his immovable assets in the name of a trust, and be sued, the fact that the immovable asset is still located in the U.S. makes it vulnerable to the claims of the individual's creditor. For example, a court may disregard the transfer, especially if there is a fraudulent transfer issue, and have the property re-deeded or re-titled in the name of the creditor. The only way to make an immovable asset unattractive to a creditor is to remove its value. Removing value, by a mortgage or lien, and placing that value (proceeds of the mortgage or loan) into an offshore trust in effect protects the immovable asset from the claims of creditors.

In your experience, do you find that a single entity or strategy is sufficient for most people, or do you commonly recommend a multi-layered structure?

In my experience, keeping it simple is the best way to protect most individuals. If the structure is simple, the client is able to understand how it works and is more inclined to keep the integrity of the structure. If an individual has sufficient wealth, an offshore trust is always the preferred core structure. The use of one trust that is properly drafted, structured, and implemented is most often sufficient. That one trust, in turn, may hold other entities in order to contain potential liabilities. Multi-layered structures may be used to confuse potential claimants, but they also confuse clients, lead to claims of piercing the corporate veil, and make the litigating attorneys richer. The single strategy that works is the use of an offshore trust.

CASE STUDY: PATRICIA DONLEVY-ROSEN

Have you found that you have needed to change your methods in recent years, because of FTC v. Affordable Media, or to include Nevis LLCs?

In recent years, as a result of FTC v. Affordable Media, a client's spouse can no longer serve as the trust protector. Unlike the poorly drafted trust in Affordable Media, we have never permitted our clients to be the trustee or the protector of their trusts.

The case, however, has been useful to show clients why our trust provisions restricting control are needed in order to assure protection of their assets.

Affordable Media also helped us to explain to our clients why all trusts are NOT created or drafted equally. Many offshore trust companies offer trust forms, and these are often used by U.S. lawyers who are not well-versed in offshore asset protection planning. If the particular offshore legislation permits, these forms will provide protective provisions such as a flight clause and a duress clause; however, such form language will fail to provide for the effective execution of the clauses. For example, most flight clauses provide that the trust may move to another jurisdiction, if appropriate without providing a mechanism to be certain that the flight clause can be effected under all circumstances (for example, even if an injunction has been issued). Also, most forms of duress clauses nullify the attempted exercise of any power unless exercised by the power holder of his/her own free will — again, without providing a mechanism by which the trustee can be certain that a power is being freely exercised. Usually it is only counsel with extensive experience with offshore trusts who have thought out and provided for all contingencies.

Some people have offshore trusts drafted by non-U.S. lawyers or other professionals located in the offshore jurisdiction. Although these persons may address protective clause issues, they will uniformly fail to draft a trust document providing for the optimum legal tax and estate planning under U.S. laws. For example, they rarely provide for the marital deduction or credit shelter trusts-thus, possibly resulting in gift taxes and higher than necessary estate taxes.

CASE STUDY: PATRICIA DONLEVY-ROSEN

Briefly describe a "success" story, that is, an asset protection plan that was threatened in some way and withstood the attack, and why. Please change names as you think fit.

We have plenty of these.

One involved parents of a teenager that had an accident with the father's car, where the mother had signed the state's form agreeing to be responsible for the acts of the teenager. The father's assets, the mother's assets, and the couple's joint assets (in this case held as tenants by the entirety) would have all been subject to the claim of the injured parties. However, the parents had recently completed their estate planning, which used an offshore trust. All the parents' liquid assets were in the trust, their real estate interests had been stripped of any equity, and there was nothing to gain. The matter was settled for the insurance policy limits.

Another case involved a client, Aries, who was threatened by an irate ex-wife who wanted to take away his most precious possession just to emotionally hurt him — his sports memorabilia. However, the memorabilia was owned by an LLC that had borrowed against the value of the memorabilia, pledged it, and put the proceeds in Aries' offshore trust. The court told the ex-wife there was nothing that could be done.

Felix, another client, sued by Willow for date rape. He had his assets in offshore trust, and his real estate had been stripped of equity. He settled the case for a small sum, compared to what Willow was after.

In another example, Todd earned a fortune taking Internet companies public. Before the Internet bubble burst in 2000, he transferred his profits to an offshore trust with an offshore bank account. After the bubble burst and many shareholders lost money, class actions and SEC claims followed. While the various litigations went forth Todd and his family were able to continue enjoying their luxurious lifestyle, as the offshore trustee paid all their expenses. The class actions and SEC investigations all eventually went away, either being dismissed or settled.

CASE STUDY: PATRICIA DONLEVY-ROSEN

Briefly describe an unsuccessful story where assets were seized — this may well be the story of someone who came to you for advice after the lawsuit. Please change names as you think fit.

Susan was entering a second marriage with a small fortune from her deceased husband.

Her future husband Fred was at odds with his siblings. Susan talked to us about asset protection, then decided she didn't need to do anything as she had nothing to do with Fred's siblings, their dispute, and intended to keep her money separate, in accordance with their pre-nuptial agreement. When the siblings got a judgment that they could not collect from Fred, a court allowed them to garnish an account of Susan's, an account that was easily traceable to her deceased husband. It was too late to do anything at this point.

Harry, another example, sold a business and with the profits funded an offshore trust, drafted by a reputable and esteemed firm. Years later, he separated from his wife, and was ordered to pay his wife support on a monthly basis. He did so out of his U.S. funds. When that money ran out, a U.S. court ordered him to ask the offshore trustee to make payments. Properly, the trustee refused. Harry would have been protected. However, the trust had a U.S. bank account which the wife's attorney found out about. The funds out of that bank account were seized. An example as to why the funds need to be offshore in an institution with no U.S. connection.

If relevant, what changes did you recommend to improve the asset protection in this last case?

These were not clients for whom we did trusts, but we use their stories to show clients what can go wrong if action isn't taken and taken properly to protect assets.

ASSET LOCATION

Just because you have settled on a certain country for your legal structure to provide the asset protection and tax position that you want, that does not mean your trust's assets have to be in that country. All that is necessary is that the assets are titled in the trust's name, which means that all paperwork will need to be routed through and signed by the trustee for deposits and disposals.

Perhaps you might think that it would be convenient to keep the assets in the United States. It could, but this is not a recommended location for a couple of reasons. Firstly, imagine the position of the investment company that holds your assets in the name of the trust, should they receive a court order requiring your assets to be frozen or passed over in satisfaction of a judgment. While the trust is set up so you do not have personal ownership of the assets and they should be safe, it would only take a slip up, or a junior being handed the task, for them to be seized. It is better if they are totally out of the reach of the United States judicial system.

The other reason to hold them abroad is to gain diversity in your investments. If you hold some of your assets in one or more other currencies you will automatically have your portfolio hedged against a continuing failing in the economy.

The next most obvious place to have the assets located is in the country where your trust has been established. In that way, the trustee will have easier control and be able to simply follow the trust's requirements for distributing income and reinvesting assets. Even this may not be as safe as you would think, because of a legal precedent called the Mareva injunction, which was established in the Cook Islands in 1975, and has also been referenced and granted in other jurisdictions. The case involved a company called Mareva Compania Naviera S.A., which is where the name derives.

This applies particularly to the challenge of a fraudulent conveyance, that is, an asset relocation that is done with the intent to cheat the creditor. As I mentioned previously, even if this has been upheld in the U.S. legal system, it would have to be tried again and proved in the foreign jurisdiction for the claimant to have a legal right to seize the assets. There are obstacles to this succeeding, such as the statute of limitations which requires the case to be brought speedily, and the different criteria applied to proving the transfer was fraudulent, such as proof beyond a reasonable doubt which is required in many foreign jurisdictions.

Nonetheless, whether the fraudulent conveyance case ultimately succeeds, the Mareva injunction can be inconvenient. What would happen, and did happen in the Cook Islands, is that a local attorney would go to the court and file for a Mareva injunction. He does not have to wait until the trial, and he does not have to tell the trustee or anyone else that he is going. When the Mareva injunction is granted it instructs the trustee not to take any action that would in any way affect the ability for the creditor to gain access to the funds, should the case subsequently be proved. In other words, it puts a freeze on the trust's assets until the case has been determined.

This means the trustee cannot relocate the assets, he cannot sign anything that changes the way they are held, and he cannot even resign. Everything stays as it is until the time that the case is proved or dismissed. How likely is the trustee to obey this instruction? Very likely, as he relies on keeping his license as a trust company for his livelihood and it has been established to be a legal action in the country in question. Incidentally, the Supreme Court of the United States established in 1999 that a similar injunction could not be granted in U.S. courts, as it departed from American principles of equity.

REAL ESTATE

You may be wondering if there is any way that a foreign trust can hold real estate for asset protection — in this case, we are particularly concerned about real estate in the United States. This would seem at best to be awkward, and in practice does not usually work out. Real estate counts as real property, which is physically related to a certain country or state; trust are better suited to protect personal property which by its nature can be located in different places.

With real property, most states have rules that require the courts to apply the laws of the property's actual location. Whether you argue that a foreign trust holds title, the fact is that the property is under the judge's nose, and that means he has in rem jurisdiction, a legal term meaning that he can still have some control over the asset because it is within his district. He can, for instance, simply sign over the property to the creditor on this basis.

FOREIGN BANK OR CORPORATION

It is simple to open a foreign bank account, and it sounds like a much easier proposition than forming a trust, so why would you not take this simple course? After all, the use of Swiss bank accounts, famously only identifiable by number and not by name, has long been accepted as a way to hold your wealth anonymously.

On a point of information, it is not quite as simple to open a Swiss bank account nowadays as it used to be. The minimum deposit is typically $100,000, and that prevents many people from giving it due consideration. That aside, apart from indulging in illegal activity, there is no real protection from creditors by having an account in Switzerland. The key to the Swiss success is that it routinely provides financial privacy to the rich, but that is not the same thing as asset protection.

Provided the foreign bank does not have branches in the United States, which can compromise the position, it does not have to respond to any court orders originating in the United States. It does not have any legal relationship to this country. However, if you have a bank account over which you have control, you would have to reveal it at a debtor's exam. The debtor's exam is when a judgment has been granted, and you are placed under oath and asked about your assets. You commit perjury if you lie about these assets. Asset protection is about placing assets so that creditors cannot legally touch them, and not necessarily about just making them hard to trace, as the debtor's exam will cut through the obfuscation. Your Swiss bank will not respond to a court order, but you have to or be held in contempt, and put in jail.

Again, only you and the IRS would know of your bank account. You have additional paperwork to file with the IRS if you control funds worth more than $10,000 in a foreign account, and while this does not attract additional taxes, you must declare it to ensure that the IRS does not suspect that you are engaged in nefarious activities, and start an investigation. As it is, you may find that you are more likely to be selected for an audit by such diversification.

If you choose not to use a foreign bank account, then why not consider a foreign corporation to protect your assets? In respect to a normal corporation formed in a foreign country under the foreign law, this may work to some extent, but suffers from the same problem as a foreign bank account, in that you control the company and hence, its assets. In the same way as a judge has jurisdiction over you and can order you to turn over your assets from the bank account, he can make you turn over the corporations assets too, and you refuse at your peril as you will be held in contempt of court. You have introduced more complication to comply with the laws of the country and not achieved the desired effect.

NEVIS LLC

Not a foreign trust, but a limited liability company, the Nevis LLC has become an interesting prospect for asset protection in recent years. Offshore trusts have been widely used for asset protection, but it seems that the Nevis LLC may be set to overturn that old favorite, as it potentially provides more protection at a lower cost.

Nevis is a small island in the Caribbean, and has been on the foreign asset protection radar since the 1990s, when it revised its laws to become more attractive to the multibillion-dollar business opportunities. The statutes were to some extent modeled on the Delaware legislation, but sought to include as many improvements as could be devised to make it the country of choice for U.S. citizens seeking offshore asset protection.

While the Nevis LLC is modeled on the American legislation, they have taken the opportunity to include features that you simply cannot get under American laws. You have seen in the LLC chapter that an LLC is a separate legal entity and there is no personal liability for members and managers beyond a charging order remedy. You have a choice of a member-directed or an actively managed LLC, and for asset protection you would choose the latter, with a foreign manager. As always, you do not want to have enough control that you are able to forcibly repatriate the assets, as you could be directed by the court to do that.

As stated, the Nevis LLC has the charging order remedy, which mirrors that available in the United States. With a manager in control, the charging order remedy is available to creditors, but they have to prove their case in the Nevis courts. The manager will correctly ignore any such order from a foreign jurisdiction, such as the United States. Note also that Nevis has worked in some features not available in the United States to make it a more desirable option for asset protection.

For instance, the Nevis laws insist that anyone challenging a transfer to a Nevis entity, which would also include a Nevis trust, has to employ a local lawyer to argue their case. More than this, the modus operandi of many lawsuit attorneys in this country is to work on contingency. That is tempting for the plaintiff, as it means they do not have to pay the costs for a case that does not produce any reward. It is a lucrative way of working for the attorney, provided he picks his cases well, as he stands to pick up typically around half of the award. This is not allowed in Nevis; the lawyer must be directly hired and not work on contingency, making it a much more difficult proposition for the claimant.

Again, this does not mean that a member of the Nevis LLC cannot have funds released to their account. The charging order only applies to a distribution of profits or to liquidation distributions that would normally come to the member. It does not limit, for example, the payment of a salary, or of a loan from the LLC to the member. If you are wondering how you can legitimately earn a salary on a foreign corporation when you are not even in the country, consider that you are probably advising the manager on where you want the assets invested. This would make you a financial adviser for the LLC, and thus fairly claiming a salary for your expertise.

However, in certain cases, you can find that the creditor incurs a tax liability on the profits of the LLC, even when they have not been distributed, and thus a charging order remedy can be a disadvantage to the creditor. This is similar to the idea expounded in the limited trust section — you have a "profit," even though it is not paid out, and therefore you, or the creditor in your place as this is where they have positioned themselves, is liable for taxes on that profit.

It can be a good idea to have more than one member of the LLC, and requiring that all members have to agree before the manager can be changed. In practical terms, this means the United States court cannot require you to replace the manager with one who is sympathetic to the creditor, which is otherwise a weakness that might be exploited. The manager can also be under the continued instruction of a duress clause, which requires him not to pay out if he knows that you are being forced to ask for the assets.

One additional feature of Nevis LLC asset protection is that you can transfer assets to the LLC even after you already have an existing creditor, and it will not be regarded as a fraudulent transfer. The Nevis ordinances allow this to take place if the member's interest can be claimed to be in proportion to the amount contributed, and the rules on this are in favor of the investor. Basically the fair value argument is applied, but with some twists.

Just a few further benefits include that Nevis does not require the amount of record keeping needed for an LLC under United States law, for instance meetings are not needed, and the cost is generally less than using a foreign trust. If you are considering a Nevis LLC, you should ensure that your advisers include someone who is fully familiar with this entity.

OFFSHORE INSURANCE

The topic of offshore insurance is not one that you will find in every description of tools for asset protection and with good reason — it is only for major wealth protection, and is comparatively expensive. If you have a need for it though, there are significant tax and protection benefits.

This would be a business that makes a profit of $300,000 or more. Christopher Jarvis and David Mandell in their book Wealth Secrets of the Affluent consider that setup costs are around $100,000, and annual costs about $50,000. So you can see that the offshore insurance company is not for everyone.

Captive insurance companies (CICs) are adopted for their tax benefits as well as their asset protection abilities. They must be registered with the IRS and also licensed to write insurance in the United States, although they are formed typically in Bermuda or the British Virgin Islands, as these jurisdictions are favorable to insurance companies in terms of their laws. Arnold Goldstein in *So Sue Me!* estimates that more than one-third of commercial insurance is actually written by offshore CICs, with $60 billion in premiums each year, and this number is increasing. It used to be only the large companies that took on this task, but in the last few years it has been increasingly the realm of small business owners and professionals.

This is much more than just an asset protection tool. It is quite literally insurance for your business against malpractice claims and other issues for which you as a professional may find that your business is liable. As such, it is applicable if you are in a profession that would normally consider it prudent to have professional liability insurance. With the correct structure you need not be concerned that you will be left holding all the liability as though you had never taken out insurance, as it is common for your insurance company to transfer some risks to a reinsurer to avoid having risk.

The premiums that you pay to your own insurance company are tax deductible as a business expense, just as when you are using an outside company. To the extent that you are not reinsuring the risk, you would pay out minor claims from this money, again with pretax funds. The funds that are not used in this way, or for reinsurance with another company for calamitous claims, are invested and can build in a tax-free way. On the other hand, they are only liable to long-term capital gains taxes should you decide to reclaim them.

The insurance company must be established and run in accordance with the standards and requirements to enable it to be recognized by the United States; this is needed to ensure the tax benefits. The company has to be financially viable for this purpose, so that it cannot be dismissed as a sham for the purpose of asset hiding only; but other than that it can be managed quite flexibly. One way of managing it is to cover the lower payouts from your own company, and use commercial insurance with a much higher deductible to cover major claims. This commercial insurance would therefore be much more reasonably priced.

In terms of asset protection, your premiums are protected from creditors, just as if you were insuring with another company. The premiums are paid for a service, and are not available as your direct assets any more. Your professional liabilities are also covered by the protection, so that the capital, which is to cover this, will be protected. This is a case of you still having control of your assets, but not being able to be forced to repatriate them to satisfy a creditor, as they are not assets of your business that is being sued.

You can set up the insurance to provide just the items that you want. For instance, you can customize the coverage to cover legal fees for defense with any attorney you want, but to not allow the funds to be claimed by a creditor. It is your insurance company, and you can tailor the terms in any reasonable way.

In review, this is in some ways like having a fund set aside for contingencies and emergencies, but it is much more efficient. Instead of being taxed on the money that you put into the fund, you pay the premiums tax-free. Instead of having the fund subject to attack from creditors, it is protected.

Should you feel that this is a suitable vehicle for your purposes, you must make sure it is set up by experts in establishing CICs. While it has terrific potential to provide excellent asset protection and tax avoidance, it must be correctly created and maintained. You should have a review of your affairs to determine the suitability, from which you can make a valued judgment of whether the captive insurance company is for you.

CHAPTER

11 Your Personal Residence

"Mid pleasures and palaces though we may roam, Be
it ever so humble, there's no place like home."
– John Howard Payne

Your home is probably the most important and expensive
possession in your life. To lose it to a creditor does not
bear thinking about, but think about it you must, if only
to determine the best plan to provide protection from losing it.
There are a number of ways that you can arrange your affairs to
shield the family house from seizure, and some of these involve
concepts covered earlier in the book. This chapter brings them all
together, pointing out the differences and you can check back in
the earlier chapters for more details of the particular technique.
This will allow you to directly compare the pros and cons, so you
can make a valued judgment of what suits your circumstances.

TYPES OF TITLE

But before we look at various entities that could take title and
help to protect your home, the first consideration is how you can

take title as a person, and what each way means for you. This is after all the way that the vast majority of personal real estate is held in this country.

Homes are often held between spouses as joint tenants with right of survivorship. This seems to be a logical way, as it means if one partner dies the other automatically holds the whole property. The property does not have to go through probate, and there is no share that might be willed to someone else. The house is considered as a whole, with each partner having an equal undivided interest, there is no question of splitting and selling off one share.

This is important to many couples, as on the unfortunate death of one, the other will be able to use the house or sell and move on without waiting for probate to clear, which can take some years. There is no asset protection from this arrangement, though. If one of the partners has a judgment against them, then the creditors can force the sale of the house, provided it has been held free and clear.

A second way to take title to property is as tenants in common. This is the most common form of shared ownership of a property. This means that each person has a separate fractional share in the house that can be sold or gifted to someone else. As such, if one partner is sued, the creditor can seize part of the property. In practice, this could even mean that the house would be partitioned, and the innocent partner would have little right to prevent something happening.

It does not even work for estate purposes, as there is no automatic transfer of ownership to the spouse, and the property has to go through probate, and be subjected to the will or intestacy laws if there is no will. There is no asset protection from tenants in common, except that the whole house will not be seized, and the spouse's share will be retained if only one is sued, with unintended and possibly unpredictable consequences.

In some states there is a provision to hold property as tenancy by the entirety, which is less common, and originates from the English law. This arrangement can only be between married couples, unlike the previous option. The partners do not own the property individually, but the property is owned by the entirety, that is, both of them together.

This option is available in Alaska, Arkansas, Delaware, Florida, Hawaii, Illinois, Indiana, Kentucky, Maryland, Massachusetts, Michigan, Mississippi, Missouri, New Jersey, New York, North Carolina, Oklahoma, Oregon, Pennsylvania, Rhode Island, Tennessee, Vermont, Virginia, Wyoming, and the District of Columbia — just about half of the states. It is considered a better option than the previous two, although it is no real safeguard on its own.

Each state has a slightly different interpretation of the application of this ownership, but usually it protects the innocent spouse's share of the house from creditors. The right of survivorship cannot be severed, even though one share of the house can be sold as a right to use the property during the seller's lifetime.

The problems with tenancy by the entirety include that if there is a claim on both spouses, there is no asset protection at all and if a spouse dies or you get divorced during the lawsuit, you lose all protections. But, it is a possible way of holding property, if combined with other safeguards.

HOMESTEAD EXEMPTION

In the chapter on exemptions, there are details about what was available, and its limitations, which included the fact that for most states the exemptions were woefully inadequate compared with today's values. Also remember that the homestead exemption does not usually prevent the loss of your home for what can be gleaned from it — all it means is that when the home is sold, you are given the amount of the exemption out of the proceeds.

Just five states give you complete homestead protection, one of these being Florida where O.J. Simpson sits in defiance of the claims on him. But five states give you no homestead exemption at all. Most states give you from $5,000 to $50,000 in protection, although a few give you six-figure coverage. In most cases, the homestead exemption is nearly worthless, and while you can and should check what your state covers you will probably need to do something else to gain proper asset protection of your home.

While Florida and Texas, for example, have unlimited exemptions, note that there have been federal law changes that limit the homestead exemption to $125,000 if you have moved within 40 months of filing bankruptcy. The federal laws on bankruptcy changed recently, as you may remember, and this was one of the provisions to prevent last minute changes to shield possessions from creditors.

While you are checking on the amount that your state covers under the homestead exemption, you should also confirm any other conditions. Even if you are in an unlimited coverage state, there can be limitations on the size of property protected, as well as time restrictions. Some states provide automatic coverage, and in others you have to file with the state to claim the homestead exemption. You will need to determine who should file, as some jurisdictions only allow the head of household to submit the filing.

Further problems with relying on the homestead exemption include that some states do not even recognize a transfer of your home to a living trust, even though many estate planners routinely recommend this course of action to avoid probate. Homesteading is also not effective against certain creditors, such as the government and the mortgage company. In general, you often will not find that a homestead exemption can protect you to any great extent, even though it serves as another hurdle for a creditor to have to deal with,

LIMITED PARTNERSHIP

In contrast, the limited partnership is a viable tool and sometimes recommended for protecting your home. It may not be the best for your situation, but it warrants some consideration. The treatment of the tax deduction for mortgage interest and the capital gains tax exemption of $250,000 ($500,000 for a couple) on a sale is an issue though, as it can be for other holding entities.

It is important to note that the limitation with a limited partnership is that it has to have a general partner, who is still exposed to all liabilities and charges. The way that the impact of this is often minimized is by having a corporate entity as the general partner. The general partner will frequently not hold a large percentage of the company, as this is not required to be in the managerial position of general partner, and this further reduces the exposure.

It is true that there are differing views of the efficacy of the limited partnership for home protection. Some say that the use of limited partnerships and limited liability companies provides the "greatest asset protection possible," like Sharon Lechter and Garrett Sutton in the guide *Rich Dad's Real Estate Advantages*, Rich Dad's (Robert Kiyosaki's) advisers. On the other hand, Christopher Jarvis and David Mandell in *Wealth Secrets of the Affluent* assert that they "no longer recommend single-owner LLCs and FLPs to protect the family home."

The argument that can be advanced against the limited partnership, and for that matter corporations and LLCs, is that they are companies, and are supposed to be used for a business. The family home has no good reason to be held in a business entity, and the creditors can post an effective argument to the judge that the organization is nothing but a sham, designed to hide assets from seizure. Particularly the case when the business has a single owner, this argument has been upheld for an LLC when the protections were set aside by a recent court decision.

CORPORATION

A further option for holding property is a corporation, but this is in many ways inferior to a LP or LLC. If you try using a C-corporation, you will quickly run into tax disadvantages that will convince you that you have made the wrong choice.

Consider that you may have capital gains on your property, as this is the expected normal course of events. With a C-corporation, you have to pay corporate taxes first on your profits. The remainder is then taxed as a dividend to the shareholders, which may leave around half the gain intact.

Note that there is an alternative choice with a corporation, and that is to have an S-corporation, where you can elect to have the corporation as a pass-through tax entity in which no corporate tax is paid. In this respect, the tax payable on a capital gain would generally be the same as with a LP or a LLC. But there are no advantages from using an S-corporation. The disadvantage that if you wanted to remove the property from the entity, the S-corporation would require taxes to be paid that would not apply with a LP or LLC.

LIMITED LIABILITY COMPANY

As detailed previously, the limited liability company or LLC is an entity that overcomes perceived issues with other existing business forms. The issue of taxation is one, where the LLC allows you to have a full pass-through to your personal taxes of any profits. The LLC also allows you to have a single member, so that you can have the idea and protections of a partnership with only one owner. That is the theory, at least.

In practice, it has not worked out quite as well as expected. The single member LLC has been challenged solely for evading creditors, and there are now a few adverse court decisions on the record. This is not to say that the LLC is not a beneficial entity to use as part of your asset protection and estate planning, but just to emphasize that you need to set up your overall financial structure with care and using experts in their fields, and even then do not expect it to be bulletproof against all claims forever. Your best protection is to make it exceedingly difficult and somewhat uncertain for any would-be creditor so that they may think twice about putting in the effort for little return.

Note that in California, there have been some cases that have dismissed the protection of the LLC, and a bankruptcy case in Colorado has also called the expected protections into question. These cases can be cited in other jurisdictions to try to influence the court's decisions, but are already precedents in the named states.

That said, this entity may be on balance the one that you decide to use, so here are the answers to some other questions that you may have concerning real estate held by an LLC.

When you are buying a property in your own name, you can take the mortgage interest as an itemized deduction when preparing your personal taxes. It is true that some courts have held that the deduction does not apply to entities, and is only valid for individuals. Many accountants now use a single member LLC, which is disregarded for tax purposes, to pass through the deduction to your personal return, and you should confirm with your accountant whether this is the interpretation that has been accepted in your area.

If part of your asset protection plan is to rely on the homestead exemption, then you should note that in many states, the exemption is only permitted for individuals or sometimes couples. This will be set out in your state statutes. If you are considering having your home held by a business entity, you would be wise to ensure that your plan does not require any protection from the homestead exemption.

If you are re-titling your residence, you may be concerned that you can trigger the due-on-sale clause of your mortgage. This can be ignored by many people, and normally it is not noticed. As long as the mortgage is paid reliably and on time, then the lender may not have reason to find out. There is a law that allows you to transfer the title to a living trust for estate planning purposes, and it is possible to argue to your lender that it is a similar process to re-title to another type of entity, and that it should therefore be permitted. Often this will work, but it may also depend on what the interest rates are. For example, if the rates are higher now than the existing mortgage the lender may be keen to see the property refinanced.

Finally, does the protection of title insurance continue to apply with a title change? This can be subject to interpretation, and you should review the terms of your title insurance. This will be more likely to continue if you change the title using a grant deed rather than a quit-claim deed.

LIVING TRUST

The living trust is the most popular trust, and is frequently recommended for estate planning purposes. It can avoid the delays and the cost of probate, but as a revocable trust, it does not provide much asset protection. Because you can change the terms at any time, you are also able to gain access to your assets, and may be ordered by the court to do so. If you refuse, you will be held in contempt, and can be put into jail if you refuse.

As also pointed out in the earlier chapter dealing with trusts, the living trust can also jeopardize the homestead exemption. Frequently you will find that this disadvantage is not fully explained by those estate planners who advocate using this entity for its admitted advantages.

QUALIFIED PERSONAL RESIDENCE TRUST

This is a special trust particularly designed for holding your house, and gives a great way to reduce the taxes on the estate, as well as providing asset protection. As an irrevocable trust, the asset protection is good because you have no way of recapturing the assets and so cannot be forced to do so by the courts. It does not protect the asset from a claim on the beneficiary, though.

The usual term for the trust is ten years before the asset is given to the beneficiaries, and you may be wondering where this comes from. It is tied up in the tax saving possibilities of the trust, together with your anticipated lifespan. This type of trust is also available for a second home, though not for rental properties, on which you would claim depreciation.

You are probably aware that there is a limit on how much you can give away in your lifetime before you are taxed on the gift. This is to prevent you from giving all your goods to your offspring on your deathbed, and avoiding inheritance tax entirely.

The limit is adjusted from time to time, and at the moment is $1,000,000 total in a lifetime. If you have a home worth $1.2 million, for example, you would have to pay gift taxes on $200,000 if you were to give it away to your children right now. As an alternative, if you put your home in an irrevocable trust, a QPRT, the gift does not count as worth that much. The value would be determined from IRS tables, and these are based on the fact that the gift that you have to wait ten years to get is not worth so much now — in fact, the tables tell us it is only worth about a half-million dollars. That means you have not used up your lifetime gift tax exemption, and can even give more without paying the tax.

If the term of the trust was 15 or 20 years, the value from the tax tables would be even lower, giving more room for passing on assets without incurring tax. The only question that you have to answer is how long you expect to live. If you die before the trust ends, then the process was in vain, and the house goes back into the estate to be taxed.

LAND TRUST

You may recall that the land trust does not have a great deal going for it. The estate planning issues can be matched by a simple living trust, which can include other assets. The major feature of the land trust is that it prevents easily determining who the owner of the property is. Usually a bank will be the trustee, and your name will not appear on the records. To the extent that making assets hard to find can help asset protection, this may be helpful, but given that you are living in the house, the records may well be pieced together and traced back to you. For instance, you probably owned the land before granting it to the trust, so the real relationship may be obvious.

This is in contrast to the assertions that may be made by advocates of the land trust, who maintain that it truly hides the identity of the owner. Other claims include that it has certain asset protection, saves taxes, and avoids triggering a due-on-sale clause on selling the property.

SHIELDING BY DEBT

Have you reached that amazing moment in your life when you pay off your mortgage and proudly hold your home free and clear? It gives you a tremendous feeling of satisfaction, and, curiously, considering how vulnerable you actually are, a sense of security. That is, it would have given you those feelings if you had not read this book to this point; now, it would probably fill you with dread to realize how exposed you are.

For many people, paying down their mortgages and reducing the regular outgoings is one of their goals. Therefore, it is counterintuitive to burden yourself with debt on the property; but the truth is, it is one of the best ways of dissuading a creditor to seek to take your home. After all, why would a creditor force the sale of your house if the bank would have to be paid back, taking most of the money? Quite possibly the remainder of the money would be covered by the homestead exemption, leaving the creditor with nothing and no reason to try.

With the sub-prime crisis, falling values, and rising foreclosure rates, many people who have not been homeowners for long are finding that their mortgages are upside-down — they owe more on their house than they could sell it for. Every cloud has a silver lining, and although the majority of them do not realize it, they have an excellent asset protection in place automatically for their house. If the mortgage was affordable before the decline in value, and there have not been any changes to their income, then it is still affordable and the best option is to keep on paying it, and not worry about paper losses. After all, provided they do not have to move, the market will stabilize in a few years and house prices start going up again.

It is interesting to note that the representatives of insurance and securities firms have been forbidden to recommend borrowing from your home to fund investments. The advisors have not even been permitted by their companies to take the proceeds from refinancing into their schemes. Perhaps the sub-prime and credit crisis would have had an even larger impact if this restriction was not in place, but this strategy should be used by knowledgeable investors with wealth that needs sheltering and therefore would not have added to the foreclosure numbers.

A simple way of putting this idea into practice is to arrange a home equity line of credit, or HELOC, with a lender. This can often be done free of charge with your mortgage company, as they will already have an appraisal on your property. You should aim that the amount available leaves little or nothing for a creditor to take away from a forced sale. Although the money has not been borrowed, there is a lien, or note, against your house for the amount, which may deter creditors.

For further security, you will need to actually borrow the money, paying the interest, and invest it in an asset protected way to earn as much as you can safely. This technique will cost you the difference in interest each year, but provides even better protection than just having the availability of the debt.

CHAPTER 12

How Well
Do You Know
Your Spouse?

"Nearly all marriages, even happy ones, are mistakes: in the sense that
almost certainly (in a more perfect world, or even with a little
more care in this very imperfect one) both partners
might be found more suitable mates."
– J.R.R. Tolkien

It is sad but true; many marriages are end in divorce, and there is a real risk that you may have more than one divorce in your lifetime. Your ex-spouse may prove to be more of a risk to your assets than a disgruntled creditor, and to leave out protection of your assets from this threat is to leave a gaping hole in your planning. You will also be concerned at how much your marital partner's independent actions can lead to a claim on your resources, and the answer to this is not straightforward.

This is not to suggest that you should intend to deprive your "ex" of any share of your joint estate, but if you have the necessary structures in place to prevent assets being taken by the force of a court order, you can negotiate a reasonable settlement from a position of strength. In fact, the best and most equitable planning will result from the two of you discussing the possibility and deciding on an agreement that would cover the situation. If relationships have broken down to the extent that a divorce is contemplated, the emotional atmosphere may prevent much rational discussion taking place. The only winners will be the divorce lawyers who will rapidly spend down your wealth.

In the realms of planning for divorce, also include planning for your children. This could prevent a partner in marriage who turns out in time to be a gold digger from taking your money and their inheritance.

The number one problem in marriage is money, and it is also the number one cause of divorce. It is a somewhat clinical idea, but if you discuss and implement a prenuptial agreement in advance it will assist greatly if things do not work out long term.

THE DEFAULT POSITION

Often asset protection has been approached from the point of view that you own one thing, and your spouse owns another. For instance you may each have an auto that you usually drive, and you may think that this distinction would carry through if there is a claim on your property, particularly if you have titled the property in that way. This is not always the case, as many states have statutes that share the assets between two spouses. Nine states have community property laws: Arizona, California, Idaho, Louisiana, Nevada, New Mexico, Texas, Washington, and Wisconsin. Alaska allows spouses to decide to have community property if they wish. Every other state is a separate property state.

This has ramifications on your asset protection planning. For example, in a separate property state, your creditors generally have no claim to the separate property of your spouse, which is decided by whose name is on the property title. This is why you will sometimes see the recommendation to title everything in your spouse's name, so that you, with a high-risk job, will not lose everything to a lawsuit. Of course, this tactic would work against you in the case of divorce, and you will want to explore the alternative asset protection strategies outlined in this book.

In a similar way, your creditor cannot claim any of your spouse's earnings in settlement of the debt. Provided that the claim is related solely to your actions, his or her money will be detached from any settlement. It may not always be a clear-cut case of one person's liability or another. For instance, if you hold a rental property jointly, and some accident arises on the property that results in a claim, then you will both be subject to the lawsuit. You need to carefully determine where the risks are, and title your assets appropriately. In a separate property state, it is common to make an assessment of which spouse has most exposure to risk, and to title the assets in the name of the lower risk spouse.

There are some exceptions to the rule of separate liabilities, for example when a debt is incurred for necessities such as food or medical care the courts will often decide that the spouse's assets can also be seized. This will depend on the jurisdiction together with any established case law.

In a community property state, any possessions that you acquire after marriage are assumed to be owned by the community, which is comprised of yourself and your spouse in equal parts, so you are each in theory 50 percent owners. This is true even if the title is written to only include one of you. This applies also to any earnings that you may both have.

It does not start out this way when you get married. If you bring property into the marriage, then it is still considered yours while it is owned. If it is sold, and something else bought with the proceeds, then that may be considered solely owned. Whenever the funds are mixed, or commingled, in any way, then you lose that separate ownership. If you owned a house before marriage, but after marriage you pay the mortgage or taxes from a joint account to which you both contribute, that would be sufficient to make the house jointly owned in a community property state. This case would need to be analyzed in detail to determine each spouse's contribution to the asset, and this would keep the divorce lawyers busy for some time, but without doubt your spouse would have some financial interest in the property.

The treatment of community property even in the named states can vary wildly. California tends to place all property into the community, and this makes it available to be seized even if the liability was incurred prior to marriage. Nevada rules that the community property is split 50/50, and the spouse who was not involved cannot lose his or her share to creditors. You can see that it is necessary to look at your particular situation and state of residence to determine what measures are necessary for your best asset protection.

THE PRENUPTIAL AGREEMENT

While living in a separate property state may, on the face of it, provide the opportunity for better intrinsic asset protection, there is a mechanism to emulate this in a community property jurisdiction, removing yourself from the ramifications of the community property law. This can be achieved by entering into a prenuptial agreement in most community property states. If you are already married, then a postnuptial agreement is also allowed.

It still is not common for couples to enter into prenuptial agreements, but this is the foundation of protection from the less desirable consequences of divorce, and from unexpected results. It is a written contract. It sets out not only the disposition of assets including things like heirlooms should the marriage come to an end, but can also cover aspects of married life, such as what religion children would be raised in, and any financial expectations within the marriage.

States have their own rules regarding what is expected in a prenuptial agreement, and they differ only slightly between states. The agreement must be in writing, signed, and possibly notarized. It must take a fair account of the assets that each person has and brings to the marriage, and must be written as an even handed document, not deliberately biased on one side or the other. In fact, many states require that each person have a separate attorney to ensure a balanced position is taken.

The prenuptial agreement can take on a special purpose when one or other of the partners has been married, particularly if children are involved. The premarital agreement can waive the rights of inheritance in favor of the existing children, for instance. A well-written agreement can also separate liability even in a community property state, so that each spouse cannot be held liable for the debt of the other.

THE POSTNUPTIAL AGREEMENT

Also called a transmutation agreement, the postnuptial agreement is something that is prepared after the marriage, and is used to achieve similar asset separation purposes in community property states. However, it is unlikely that you can completely deny ownership of assets by one partner just on the basis of such an agreement. The division needs to be somewhat equitable to stand up to the courts; otherwise it will be seen to be merely a device to defraud creditors.

Most of the community property states allow some form of transmutation agreement, and you will need to get advice and check on the provisions in your circumstances. For example, in California you are allowed to transmute community property to separate property and vice-versa, but this only works against creditors if the transmutation is legally recorded. On the other hand, Nevada statutes simply allow spouses to make contracts with each other for the ownership.

Despite the benefits from a postnuptial agreement, or a prenuptial agreement for that matter, neither will properly protect assets, and you will want to consider the additional advantages of trusts or LLCs. Nevertheless, these agreements will clear the air regarding any effects of the misfortune of a divorce, and save more intense legal battles between divorce lawyers, and in that way can be said to save costs and protect assets if things do not work out between you in the long term.

CHILDREN'S DIVORCES

Regrettably, when things turn nasty, and love is replaced by hatred, civility is frequently forgotten and the combatants will go for the jugular. Thus, it could be that the charming husband your daughter found could, in a few years, be determined to take that which, reasonably, he should not be entitled to. There are many ways that this could play out. For instance, suppose your daughter's marriage turned into a disaster, and was speedily annulled, but she received a sizable inheritance while still betrothed. In a community property state, her soon-to-be-ex husband might successfully claim his half. While not equitable, this is a common scenario, in one version or another.

Your best advice would have been for her to make sure that a prenuptial agreement was in place; but no one foresaw the inheritance, so it was not separately treated in the agreement. What else could have been done differently to allow the intention to be served?

In this case, an irrevocable trust to your daughter, with a spendthrift provision, would have prevented the immediate seizure. If the money was taken out to, for instance, pay off the mortgage, it would not help the case, as the house still arguably becomes community property. The additional step of limiting the amount that can be taken out of the trust each year would have dealt with this particular circumstance. The trust fund could pay the mortgage and perhaps some bills, but the main part of the principal would still be safe and protected from the aggravated spouse. It is difficult to anticipate every circumstance that can occur, but a little forethought can make a substantial difference.

13

Do Not
Die Yet

"Many people would sooner die than think; in fact, they do so."
- Bertrand Russell

As an asset protection guide, this book would be remiss in not addressing the subject of death and the protections you should have in place to ensure that your assets can be passed on to the maximum extent possible. This comes under the general heading of estate planning, and is an intrinsic part of your overall scheme for protection. That said, the tax laws are constantly changing, and you will need to consult your tax adviser, who will be invaluable in ensuring that you plan for the current situation at the time of implementation.

The principles of the planning are fairly constant, and can involve living trusts in particular. These have been outlined in the chapter on trusts, and you will find more detail and recommendations here.

THE DEFAULT POSITION

Just because you have not explicitly set out a plan or a will for your estate at your death, do not think that there is not a plan ready for you by default. The plan may not do what you want, as it is written by your state. Under this plan, your assets will be distributed according to intestate succession, which means without a will. This amounts to a list of the family members who would benefit from your assets and is perhaps the worst situation that you can have — if no family members are found the state takes your possessions. This does not have to be the case.

The position is not only bad because you do not control who gets what, but also because your estate will have to go through probate, which the process ties up the assets and can easily take two years. Probate is a court-supervised distribution of the funds and assets by an attorney or executor, and can cost thousands of dollars. It requires the attorney to go to court to get authorization for any payments of bills or partial distribution to the heirs. This does not have to be the case.

Your estate will pay estate tax as required by law, which is the depends on the value of your estate. Before you say that your estate is not worth enough to be taxed, remember that the life insurance proceeds may be included in the estate value, even though you could not, in your lifetime, receive the funds and the insurance beneficiary is paid directly. Again, this does not have to be the case.

Federal estate tax applies on the excess amount of estate worth more than $2 million. This is not as much as it sounds, as the value of everything, with few exceptions, is included when deciding what your worth is. Even your simple life insurance policy, which is for the benefit of your wife or children, escapes probate but is included in the amounts when the IRS calculates the estate tax. With many people, actually having life insurance is the item that pushes the estate value over the limit. Life insurance is often bought with the intention of helping pay estate taxes, but ironically it makes the estate incur higher taxes.

There is also a statewide estate tax imposed in some states. Before 2001 when Congress started playing with the levels and rates, there used to be a federal estate tax credit that matched the state estate taxes, resulting in an overall tax payment that was no higher. Now, your estate will pay the state taxes in addition to an unadjusted federal tax.

At the time of writing, the amount over which you pay taxes is increasing in 2009 to $3.5 million, and then curiously estate taxes are scheduled to disappear in 2010, reappearing in 2011, unless Congress votes to make the disappearance permanent. This vagary is a result of previous tax changes, and is unlikely to remain, and your tax adviser will be aware of the current situation.

Without doubt, one of the most important things you can do is estate planning, and it has the most impact of any financial planning you do, apart from a lawsuit. Shopping around to find the most return on your investments pales in comparison to the effect of incorrect estate planning. You should also know that a simple will by itself is not estate planning and does little to save inheritance taxes or speed probate.

Many people do not even have a will, yet this is a basic document which can instruct who is to receive your assets on your death; who will see that your instructions are carried out, otherwise called the executor; and it can also include decisions about minor children. It does nothing to save any estate taxes, and it does not prevent your estate going to probate. However, your estate plan will use a type of will in conjunction with other methods to direct the disposition of assets that are not specifically named or included elsewhere.

LIVING TRUST

The details of a living trust have been explained previously, both under domestic trusts and in connection with your residence. The fact is that it offers a reduction of estate tax, avoids the delay and cost of probate, and is a good starting point for your estate planning. It should never be considered on its own if the goal is to arrange your affairs for asset protection as well as tax reduction. It is a revocable trust, and this means that you can change it and access the assets, which means a court can order them forfeit.

When you die, the trust operates to distribute your assets according to the provisions included in it, and this distribution takes place outside of probate, and according to any timing provisions that you may have included in the trust's instructions. For instance, you may have spendthrift provisions, or you may have instructed that annual payments are made to your heirs to prevent them squandering the total sum immediately.

A-B LIVING TRUST

The A-B living trust is a development from the basic living trust that is more beneficial for couples. Many couples arrange that on the first death, everything goes to the other partner — this seems reasonable, as they need to continue their lives with the benefit of the assets. Unfortunately, this may not be the best way to protect their assets from the tax man.

Married couples discover that there is an unlimited marital deduction when one spouse dies, meaning there is no estate tax when the assets are passed to the survivor. This is unfortunately as far as the research goes for many couples. There is no immediate problem, as expected, on the first death, but there can be consequences for the rest of the inheritance, when the second spouse dies.

The trouble is that if the allowed exemption, also called the unified tax credit, is not used on the death of the first spouse, then it goes away. Every individual has an allowed exemption, so a couple can have a total of double the amount if they plan carefully. If your estate is not planned so that it uses the first exemption on the first death, but just relies on the unlimited marital deduction, then on the death of the second spouse the whole combined estate has to be covered by just one exemption, and this may cause more taxes to be paid.

This is why the A-B living trust was invented. It is a revocable testamentary trust, which terms may seem a little in conflict with it being a living trust. The idea is that on the first death, the testamentary trust provision comes into action, dividing the property into two new trusts, "A" and "B." Usually trust B is assigned assets that are valued as much as the unified tax credit, and that does not go to the spouse — it is assigned to the heirs in due course, but with the condition that the second spouse can benefit from the income and interest until his or her death, when the assets will be passed on. This uses the first spouse's exemption in passing on the estate.

On the other hand, trust A is fully the second spouse's and can be revocable for his or her lifetime — the second spouse can use the assets in any way he or she wants. This trust contains the residue of the estate.

On the death of the second spouse, trust B goes straight over to the heirs. It does not matter if the value has increased to be over the exemption value in the meantime, as it was assigned in their favor when the assets were exempt. Trust A will be used to pay off debts and liabilities, and the remainder will go to the heirs, and whether it is subject to inheritance tax will depend on how much the value is. It will, however, have a full exemption on the second spouse's account, and by using this method the double exemption is used and benefited from.

IRREVOCABLE LIFE INSURANCE TRUST

The principles of this are included in the chapter about domestic trust, and it is included here as appropriate for your consideration when considering what happens on your death. It is worth repeating that this is the one means by which the proceeds of the life insurance do not get included in the value of your estate, and it is very common for the life insurance value to provide the extra worth to the estate that makes it subject to inheritance tax, if a trust is not used. This is ironic when one considers that one of the specific reasons that many people buy their life insurance is to help cover any inheritance taxes.

Fortunately, the answer to inheritance taxes of an irrevocable life insurance trust works to help with the asset protection side, too. As the trust is the owner of the life insurance policy, there is no way that the assets can be seized to satisfy the claim of a creditor. This applies equally to term life and to whole life policies, although the term life has no value unless the insured dies while the assets are under attack.

As explained in the chapter about domestic trust, this relatively easy concept for preserving and protecting the life insurance assets is specific to them, because of the gift tax which would be due on any other assets which were transferred to a trust. In fact, life insurance is possibly the only asset which we can strip out of an estate without being subject to gift taxes or inheritance taxes.

As there are some aspects of this trust which need special treatment, you would be well advised to make sure that the professional who draws up the trust for you is an expert in such things. Assuming that it is correctly drafted, you have just two important further considerations for it not to be challenged: make sure that the Crummey letter is sent every year to the beneficiaries, and make sure that you live for three years after setting it up.

14

The Alter Ego (Piercing the Veil)

"Life may change, but it may fly not;
Hope may vanish, but can die not;
Truth be veiled, but still it burneth;
Love replused — but it returneth"
- Percy Bysshe Shelley

Piercing the corporate veil involves trying to uncover the truth about the ownership of any particular asset. It can directly negate any asset protection that you thought you had from using a corporate or other entity for your business or possessions. The rules are there for good reason; if you were the injured party, then you would regard it as unfair if you could not obtain reasonable compensation from a wealthy person who happened to have his assets in a company just to elude their seizure.

Considering it from the other side, and with the number of frivolous lawsuits which are invited by our litigious society, there is also good reason that you should want to be able to protect your own assets. You would not wish to be left penniless by a trumped up lawsuit by a disgruntled ex-employee, or by a tenant who slipped on the ice, is unable to work, and blames you for not providing snow clearing. As always, there is a balance to be struck in law to ensure that the innocent are not victimized and that the guilty are punished. This book's purpose is to provide advice on protecting that which you have worked hard for, and trying to ensure the best possible security of your assets.

The courts can ignore a corporation or other entity if it concludes that the entity is the alter ego of a person or another corporation. If it is, in the court's opinion, the assets of the person can be reached to satisfy the liabilities of the entity. The alter ego theory is usually applied so that an insolvent corporation can be disregarded and the assets of a financially sound corporation reached. This could happen, for example, when someone sends up a second company in the hopes of extending their business, and that company flounders.

That situation in itself does not cause a verdict of alter ego, but the court will assess to what extent the companies are operated separately. If, for example, the insolvent company did not observe the formalities in terms of record keeping, tax filings, or a separate bank account, and quite possibly the personnel involved were the same, the court's conclusion may well be to find that the company was the alter ego, and allow creditors to access the main company to satisfy the debt.

With regard to personal asset protection, the court will look at whether there is any legitimate business conducted by the corporation, whether the funds of the corporation are commingled with personal funds, whether the corporation has purchased assets such as a company car. The court needs to satisfy itself that the corporation has been set up purely as a convenience, and is really no different in practice from the person, in which case the intended protections can be set aside. To help in the court's assessment, there are various aspects of the management and operation of the corporation that it will review in depth, and this provides guidelines which you can check to ensure that you pass the test, should it be necessary. These are the guidelines:

- Is the corporation run in a businesslike manner, and are the formalities observed? The court is entitled to question whether the proper filings were done with the state to form the corporation, whether the required meetings were held and minutes recorded, whether the regular annual reports were submitted, and so on. If the procedures have not been followed, that is a sign to the court that the business is just an alter ego.

- To what degree is the corporation run in an unlimited manner by one person? In other words, is the corporation run as if it is a genuine business, or is it run according to the whim of the owner, without keeping up with business decisions. If you don't go through the motions of getting your actions authorized on behalf of the company, but just act independently, then the purpose of the company can be questioned.

- To what extent are the corporation's actions separate from the individual? One of the most basic elements is to have a corporate bank account, and to make sure that corporate expenditure comes from there and not from your personal account. If you have other directors, and you probably should, then the decisions for the corporation's direction should be discussed and noted as such.

It is interesting to note that in Texas it is recognized that limited liability is one of the reasons that a corporation is formed in the first place, and they have a difficult standard to attain in order for the creditor to pierce the corporate veil. The Texas Business Corporation Act gives full details, and in summary the creditor has to show that the corporation was formed for the purpose of committing fraud, that it did commit the fraud, and that the fraud was to the benefit of the owner/shareholder. This means that Texas is not worried whether the corporate procedures were maintained, or even if you commingle funds. It is extremely hard to pierce the corporate veil in Texas.

It was suggested that you should have other directors as this will more clearly imply that there is a legitimate business intent to the corporation or company. A single member LLC is particularly vulnerable to being called into question, and having the corporate veil pierced. You should always try to find other members, even if they are family, although in a community property state you should make sure that your spouse completes a transmutation agreement to clarify that they have a separate interest in their membership.

15 Equity Stripping

"He that dies pays all debts"
- William Shakespeare

If you intend on living, you may be interested in avoiding payment. Equity stripping, sometimes called debt shielding, is a powerful strategy that can make you a very unlikely target for a lawsuit. The idea is to change all your unencumbered assets into debt-ridden assets that would be of very little use to a creditor. This means that in practical terms you will not be an attractive target for a court case, and this may be sufficient to make potential plaintiffs think twice.

REAL ESTATE

Equity stripping is most commonly used with real estate. Real estate is physically there, in the jurisdiction of the court, and can easily be seized. Your house may be your most valuable possession which makes it the obvious target for a large creditor. As detailed in the chapter about protecting your residence, equity stripping is an effective strategy and it works.

Jacob Stein's Success story includes a tale of successfully equity stripping.

CASE STUDY: JACOB STEIN

Mr. Stein is a partner with the law firm Klueger and Stein, LLP, in Los Angeles, California. The firm's practice is limited to asset protection, domestic and international tax planning, and structuring complex business transactions. The firm's goal is to provide the highest quality legal work that is usually associated with only the biggest law firms, in a boutique firm setting.

Stein received his law degree from the University of Southern California, and his master's of law in taxation from Georgetown University. Stein has been accredited by the State Bar of California as a Certified Tax Law Specialist and is AV-rated (highest possible rating) by Martindale-Hubbell.

In the arena of asset protection Stein assists high net-worth individuals and successful businesses in protecting their assets from plaintiffs and creditors by focusing on properly structuring asset ownership and business structures and operations. Over the course of his career, Stein has represented hundreds of clients, including: officers and directors of Fortune 1,000 companies; celebrities; Internet entrepreneurs; real estate developers, builders and investors; physicians; small business owners; attorneys, accountants and financial advisors; and many other individuals facing the adversity of a lawsuit.

Stein is also an author of numerous tax and asset protection articles and a frequent lecturer to various attorney, CPA, and other professional groups on topics ranging from asset protection to choice of entity planning, and offshore tax planning to advanced real estate exit strategies. He is an instructor with the California CPA Education Foundation, National Business Institute and Lorman Education Services, and teaches courses on advanced tax planning, asset protection, and trust law.

CASE STUDY: JACOB STEIN

He is an adjunct professor of taxation at the CSU, Northridge Graduate Tax Program. He is the past-chair of the Tax Section of the San Fernando Valley Bar Association, and a member of the tax sections of the American, California, and Los Angeles County Bar Associations.

Klueger & Stein, LLP
16000 Ventura Boulevard, Suite 1000
Encino, California 91436
Tel. 818-933-3838 • Fax 818-933-3839
jacob@lataxlawyers.com
www.lataxlawyers.com • www.maximumassetprotection.com

In what way are you involved with asset protection, and does this include general estate planning, such as for tax issues?

We have a practice that focuses exclusively on asset protection planning.

Do you specialize in any particular aspects of asset protection, such as foreign trusts or LLCs?

There is no such thing — it is a niche practice area to begin with.

In your experience, do you find that a single entity or strategy is sufficient for most people, or do you commonly recommend a multi-layered structure?

Yes, to both. For most people, a single layer of entities is sufficient, but we commonly recommend multi-layered strategies. You get to find out what is sufficient only if the structure is challenged, which happens very rarely. When you are doing the work, you try to do the most that you can, because you never know what will be needed. It is a better safe than sorry approach.

Have you found that you have needed to change your methods in recent years, because of FTC v. Affordable Media, or to include Nevis LLCs?

We have been using Nevis LLCs for many years and continue to do so until another jurisdiction comes out with friendlier LLC statutes.

CASE STUDY: JACOB STEIN

We have not changed our methods, but we constantly refine the structures that we use and how we word the LLC agreements, trusts, etc. Case law is always evolving and we update our structures to reflect that.

Briefly describe a "success" story, that is, an asset protection plan that was threatened in some way and withstood the attack, and why. Please change names as you think fit.

Dr. Mehta always encouraged his children to be entrepreneurial. So when his son undertook his first real estate development project, Dr. Mehta helped him by personally guaranteeing $1 million in loans.

Dr. Mehta was completely surprised when the real estate development went sour in April 2008 and his son began talking about a possible default on the bank loan. Mindful of the personal guaranty he signed, Dr. Mehta retained our firm for asset protection planning.

He had three primary assets: his personal residence with approximately $1 million of equity, the medical practice, and a brokerage account with approximately $700,000 of investments.

We analyzed Dr. Mehta's situation and quickly determined that for him the best course of action was to encumber his personal residence and then protect the loan proceeds. Dr. Mehta obtained a bank loan (interest only) bearing an interest rate of approximately 5.8%. Dr. Mehta then invested the loan proceeds through an offshore structure and was able to generate a 9% rate of return on his investment.

He also liquidated his investment account and moved the money offshore into the same investment structure as the loan proceeds.

We advised Dr. Mehta that it would be extremely difficult (maybe even impossible) for the bank to reach his offshore investments. It was certainly very expensive.

To equity strip is to remove the equity from your property. Your house is still as valuable, but in the simplest of cases you would have a mortgage for as much of the value as possible, and this would leave little equity for a creditor to seize. Your ideal situation for asset protection would be that you owe as much on your house as it could be sold for, making it a pointless exercise for the other side to try to take it towards your debt settlement.

You should also be aware that the Internet has made it very easy for lawyers to search for your financial profile online. They can quickly determine what real estate, businesses, cars, and boats you now own or have owned. Their search will also reveal the mortgages or liens against your property, and your goal must be to make yourself appear to be a poor candidate for a lawsuit. In fact, your assets can be claimed by other prior creditors, such as the mortgage provider, and that makes you a literally poor target.

One fairly simple way to increase the apparent debt on your house is to take out a home equity line of credit (HELOC). For the responsible borrower, this is an excellent course to take for a number of reasons, as it provides easy access to a large amount of funds at a low rate of interest which can be used in an emergency.

The one caveat is that your house can be at risk if you default on the borrowing, which is why this source should be used responsibly.

From an asset protection point of view this does not, unlike many other strategies, require specialized knowledge to implement. Your bank may be able to provide a line of credit for the cost of an appraisal, and may waive the annual fees to you as a good customer.

It is a matter of debate whether a HELOC which is not used provides secure asset protection. Certainly, many experts have declared that the mere existence of the lien on the deed discourages the lawyers from attacking this asset. After all, the public records would show that the property was encumbered for the full amount. It would take a sophisticated creditor to find out that the money was still available.

An alternative approach, which other experts advocate, is to borrow against the HELOC and put the money in a safe place, perhaps in a foreign trust, taking measures to make it secure from seizure. In this arrangement, you would typically use a safe investment that returns the best interest you can find, and it would probably cost you a certain amount each year to maintain, as the interest payable on the HELOC would usually be more than you could receive. However, as the asset is really stripped of equity, this would be more proof to attack.

One ploy which would probably not work is to wait until your assets are under threat before drawing on the equity line. If the creditor is astute enough to realize that the line of credit was not in use, he would argue that your taking the funds out constituted a fraudulent transfer, and would have a good chance of success.

An alternative to the home equity line of credit might be to have a friendly lien placed on the property, although this is less likely to withstand assault. In this case, a friend or family member would record a lien against your property. It goes without saying that you should only use someone who you trust implicitly. This method will fail unless you also have a tangible and legitimate loan attached to the process, but you could get around this by reciprocating and placing a lien for the same amount on their property. That way, you have received a value for your interest.

In truth, this process will most likely not withstand scrutiny, but it can provide a way to deter casual lawsuits on the basis that it appears you have no equity.

A third way to strip the equity from your house, but probably the least likely to succeed, is to take a lien out with an entity that you control, such as your company. This is cheaper than taking out a home equity line of credit, and less risky than asking a friend to hold a lien on your property. If there was a determined creditor, however, this is the strategy that would have the least hope of success. The purpose is simply to give the appearance that there is no equity worth chasing in your home, and a cursory examination would give that impression.

ACCOUNTS RECEIVABLE

The chapter on accounts receivable gives information about stripping out the equity on your accounts receivable. This has various advantages, but is not so easy to achieve as the equity stripping of your real estate.

There are two basic choices for an accounts receivable program. One of them is to sell your accounts receivable to a separate company, and this is called factoring. There are companies that specialize in providing this service. In essence, the factoring company buys your accounts at a discount, so you get cash up front and they work in their profit from the discount. Once the accounts are sold, you have no further connection with them, so this provides great asset protection at the expense of the discount. As you would spend time and money collecting the accounts in any case, there is an offset to the discount. Factoring is sometimes thought of as a way to improve cash flow, and indeed it is, and it also has the side benefit of asset protection.

In fact this could be implemented in a similar way to the last real estate option where you set up a company and transfer the assets, basically fulfilling your own factoring. In this case, you must pay special attention to keeping the company separate, transferring the cash between accounts and operating in a business-like manner, or you could lose an argument in court about whether the company is just an alter ego of your business. A separate reputable company would be the preferred choice.

The alternative way of accounting this is for the business to take a loan, rather than outright sell the accounting assets, using the accounts receivable for the collateral and with a lien placed on them in accordance with the Uniform Commercial Code (UCC) at the appropriate state department. As discussed previously, the loan may often be used to purchase an annuity or life insurance policy within an asset protection structure in order to provide for retirement.

The tax deductible simple interest paid for the loan is offset by the interest compounding on the annuity.

BUSINESS AND EQUIPMENT

If you have a business, it should be part of your plan to arrange your affairs not to lose what you have. You may already have a mortgage secured on the building, or loans on the equipment, and these will serve you in providing a disincentive to creditors suing you.

If you do not have loans, then you can arrange for a person or entity to place liens on the business property, and the same principles apply. The more legitimate the loans can be, the better the protection. The test of legitimacy may involve how related the person or entity is to the business, with close relationships being viewed with suspicion.

In such circumstances, it can help if you have a friendly lender. The friendly lender could be a corporation controlled by you, as an asset search would not immediately reveal that you were involved, but this structure would not resist detailed examination. You could also give the mortgage to a relative who you owed money – perhaps your father-in-law lent you money to start the business – and this would be a legitimate asset protection strategy, as the money is really not available to you to give to the creditors.

If you have a persistent creditor who still attempts to collect from your business, your friendly lender could even foreclose on your business to secure it from any approach. In his position, he has the best claim on the business, and can, by foreclosure, take away any equity. As a friendly lender, he would then sell you back your business, which would be financed with a new loan secured with a lien to him, and there would be no need for any money to change hands in order for you to be re-established and able to work.

It is quite possible that you financed your own business. From the asset protection and equity stripping point of view, there is a right way and a wrong way of doing this. The wrong way is to directly invest in your business, whether as a shareholder or providing a loan to the business. If the business fails, you would end up with little or nothing from either of these actions, and other creditors could jump ahead of you in line for what assets are left.

If you want to have priority over other creditors, your business needs to take out a mortgage with your local bank, for example. The bank would take out a lien on the business assets. Your bank may not wish to rely on this, particularly with a new business. If this is the case, you can also pledge some personal assets as collateral, and the bank would be happy to do business with you on this basis, considering its risk well covered.

If your business does not do well, the bank will be the first creditor to be paid, and can then release the lien on your personal property. Other parties who had a claim on your business cannot proceed further in their claim, as the assets of the business are gone in satisfaction of the mortgage.

CHAPTER

16

Insurance

"There are worse things in life than death. Have you ever
spent an evening with an insurance salesman?"
– Woody Allen

Up to this point, there has not been much talk about insurance. That is for a good reason. While there is a place for insurance in protecting your assets, it should not be relied upon to give blanket protection to your assets. It certainly cannot stand in the place of all the provisions mentioned previously. Many people believe that the first recourse should be the insurance company. This does not always apply, particularly if you are being sued for some professional misdemeanor, as insurance policies come with many pages of conditions and exceptions.

You cannot expect otherwise, as the insurance company is writing the terms and conditions of its risk. The size of most policy documents means that most people do not know them with anything like the depth of the company's knowledge, and you may be assured that Murphy's Law states your particular claim will be an exception.

Even if the policy does cover the claim, you may become involved in other issues such as contributory negligence, the limits of insurance for which you have paid, and even potentially bankruptcy of the insurance company. This latter case can be particularly unfortunate, as the plaintiff may have decided to sue you having determined that you had insurance. This is one of the factors that will be considered in deciding whether you are a suitable target. If the company then becomes bankrupt, the plaintiff, having invested in the lawsuit, will seek recompense directly from your assets in order to cover his time and costs.

There are two issues that aid in considering insurance coverage. The most obvious one is the policy limits. Insurance companies are understandably not prepared to allow the claim of excessive amounts, and calculate your premium by taking into account the maximum amount that you decide you should be covered for. For your part, you need to have a balance between unlimited coverage with an unaffordable premium, and too little coverage that will not meet any expected claim.

The more difficult issue to take into account is that of policy exceptions. You may want to make sure the insurance company has strict restrictions on what is covered by the policy, and they may even refuse a claim. These are within the limits if you have not filed it within a certain period of time, or followed up a phone call with a written filing. One of the items that you should check in your liability policy is whether there is a duty to defend clause. This will provide an attorney, working for the insurance company, to defend your suit. This sounds good, though you should be aware that the attorney is paid by the insurance company, and therefore will not necessarily work in your best interest if it deviates from the company's.

MOTOR VEHICLE

Your automobile insurance should have adequate limits, and if you have been insured for some time, you would be wise to make sure what they are. The liability on your car insurance should be about as much as your net worth so that the company will pay if you are sued for all you are worth. You may want to consider up to $1 million, with $100,000 being a minimum.

HOME OWNER'S INSURANCE

If you have a mortgage, then your lender will have insisted on insurance coverage and will be paying it from the escrow account. While it will cover the bank's interest, you should make sure that it covers you sufficiently for your own purposes. For instance you need liability coverage which would cover an accident to a visitor. This sort of cover is relatively cheap but not included on all policies.

The best type of policy is an all-risk policy, as the cheaper policies will not cover many events that you would normally assume to be insured.

PROPERTY & CASUALTY INSURANCE

The type of insurance that you will have for a business is called property and casualty (P&C) insurance. This is the same type of insurance that you have for your car or your house.

Property and casualty insurance should cover your legal expenses and other losses as well as the actual cost of replacing the property, or making it as it was before the loss. This is because you could be sued and win your case and still be faced with huge legal fees. This is almost unique to the American legal system. In virtually every other area of the world, if you are unsuccessfully sued you can claim your legal fees from the plaintiff. This is sometimes called the British Rule, and it works to prevent plaintiffs from suing you unless they are convinced their case has merit.

This is not so in the United States. In U.S. courts, we use what is imaginatively termed the American rule, which some would say is not as fair. The American rule states that each side pays its own legal costs regardless of the outcome of the case. That means that as a totally innocent party, you can finish up significantly out of pocket.

The reason that this rule was adopted is so that the general public would not have a barrier to suing big businesses in fear that they would adopt large expensive legal teams that would win and then demand costs. The rule allows anyone to have control of how much it will cost them to sue, and thus provide better access for the poor to be heard in court and not to be dealt with high-handedly by large corporations.

Unfortunately, it also opens the door to easy access to the legal system using contingency fee lawyers with very little downside. This means that you are much more likely to be the victim of a meritless or dubious case. If for no other reason, it means that you should consider insurance essential, even though it is not a good safeguard of your assets.

UMBRELLA LIABILITY INSURANCE

The umbrella insurance may be the most important one that you buy, even though it is not very expensive. It is designed to cover events that are not included under the specific insurances that you purchase, like if you are sued for libel. In addition, it provides further coverage that takes over where the limits are reached on the other policies. For instance, if there is a judgment for $2 million against you after a car accident, and your motor insurance limit is $1 million, the umbrella insurance will pay the extra $1 million.

Often you can get a discount on your premiums by placing all your insurances with one company, and that will ensure that the policies will fit together and work in concert where necessary. You will still need to go over the coverage amounts, incident types and exclusions with your agent to make certain that you have the coverage you want and understand the provisions.

LIFE & HEALTH INSURANCE

The other type of insurance available is called life and health (L&H), and while important to your life, it is not directly involved in asset protection. You should review the amounts every few years, as inflation erodes the values.

Your life insurance will assist your family in coping with your death and needs to be sufficient to allow your family to grow without additional problems from loss of your earnings. Health coverage should be selected with a high upper limit, even if it means that you must select a high deductible to make it affordable. The consequences of being inadequately insured in a major claim can be much more devastating to your estate than having to pay for doctor's visits.

17 Business Insiders

> "Every man has inside himself a parasitic being
> who is acting not at all to his advantage."
> – William S. Burroughs

This chapter is to warn you about a very real threat to your assets, which you can minimize with appropriate forethought. The threat is from your employees. What William S. Burroughs said about every man may be applicable to every business that has employees. Your employees may hurt you in two ways, aside from any concern that their work is not fast enough or could be more thorough.

You choose your employees carefully, as you know that they are the greatest asset that you have in succeeding in your business. Ideally, your employees come to work with an attitude of treating the business as their own, and act accordingly, taking pride in all they do. That may be the ideal, and for some it is true, but you will also find some that treat it like just a job. However, either type of employee is able to be a problem to you.

The two ways that an employee may hurt you are by direct action against you, such as a discrimination lawsuit; and by their actions, which with malice or otherwise cause a problem with the public and clients.

It is beyond the scope of this book to provide a course in human resources (HR), but you must be mindful of the consequences of your actions and inactions in dealing with your staff. You can protect yourself significantly by being careful in your selection of employee and with detailed agreements when taking him or her on to the payroll. Many legal claims arise from misunderstandings, particularly in a small business, where an employee may come to believe that he or she deserves a partnership in the business by reason of faithful work or creative contributions.

EMPLOYEE AGREEMENTS

From an asset protection point of view, you must always take care when hiring, managing, and laying off an employee. There are detailed reference books available on this topic, although you no doubt know the main points, such as non-discrimination for age or sex, when choosing your employees. When you do decide to employ someone, you will need to prepare an employment agreement or handbook to summarize your mutual understanding with regard to duties, time keeping, and other practices. Your employee handbook should be carefully considered, even though the basic text can be a boilerplate document, as each business has particular issues that need to be set out.

Your handbook must set out what are acceptable and unacceptable practices, as this may have to form the defense against an unfair dismissal case at some point in the future. If you can point to the appropriate clause, and show dismissal for cause, then any claim against you has less chance of success. Many states boast at-will employment, where termination can happen at any time. In practice, using this capacity would in many situations be dangerous and expose you to a malicious lawsuit. You must also be careful that the rules you set out in the employee handbook are reasonable.

You may want to consider a non-competition and non-disclosure section to your agreement. To be honest, it is usually difficult and expensive to try and enforce them, as the basic problem is that the then ex-employee is no longer in your pay, and yet you are trying to control his actions through the agreement. In fact, sometimes the non-competition agreement is even set aside for the simple reason that you cannot reasonably prevent someone from working for a living. Much depends on the circumstances, your state's laws, and the type of business you are in. Having the agreement in place does provide warning to the employee that you are concerned and serious about unfair competition against your business, and is often enough to stop them trying.

One area where the law will give you more support is if the employee actually tries to compete with you while he or she is still employed. This can be done by taking on casual work at the weekends or by working for a competitor in the evenings. If your agreement states that this is not permitted then you can most definitely stop them.

You are more likely to have success stopping disclosure of your trade secrets than with the competition restrictions. Most states have a version of the Uniform Trade Secrets Act (UTSA) in their statutes which allows you to sue your ex-employee and stop them from using your confidential information. Although this may be in state statute, it helps your case if the employee agreement also describes the things that you consider are to be kept secret, and require that information on these is not to be taken out of the office.

Another side of employee relations where you would be well advised to exercise care is the topic of discipline and reviews. You are inviting a wrongful dismissal case if you do not give good warning of any unacceptable work habits and ensure that the warning is in written form. This should be done without hesitation in a face to face meeting which is often called a warning interview. You need to document the problem and should take care to note both sides of the meeting. The warning should be acknowledged by the employee with a signature on the form. This signature will typically only state that the employee is aware of the contents, and will reserve his or her right to disagree, as this would make his or her refusal to sign unreasonable. The documents need to be kept in the employee's records in case it is needed if the behavior does not improve in the future.

There are many reasons that you can terminate an employee, and if several of these apply then you should take care that they are all noted in the employee's file. Apart from misconduct, you may decide on separation because the employee is incompetent or otherwise does not perform to expectations. You always able to terminate out of economic necessity, if your business has to scale down, and if this is the stated reason you should be careful that you do not employ a new person after a short time as this is a trigger for a wrongful dismissal suit.

Regarding performance reviews, you must also prepare these in a standard format, discuss them with the employee, and ask him or her to sign them as acknowledgement that they are aware of the results. Many employers also allow the employees to self-rate and to answer comments on the form which provides them with a voice on the agreed document, and can make it more palatable to them. The fact is that your comments will still stand and be witnessed by their signature. Performance reviews should be done on a regular basis, at least annually, and although many people do not relish going through this process as an employer as well as an employee, it is a necessary part of business if you are to keep control of the employment situation.

ARBITRATION AGREEMENTS

Some advisers recommend that you have a mandatory arbitration agreement with your employees. This can be all that you need to deter a former employee from starting a lawsuit with you. One of the main advantages is that it is cheaper and quicker than going through the court system. Another advantage is that there is no jury, so you do not risk the kind of case where the jury becomes emotionally attached to the plaintiff and does not necessarily submit the most secure judgment. Any award would be decided with a reasonable view to the damages incurred, in contrast to some jury awards where emotion seems to have overridden the common facts.

Arbitration is a much easier process than going to court, and consequently both parties will benefit from reduced legal fees. In fact, if you are going into business with other people, you may wish to consider having an arbitration clause for any member or shareholder agreement. An arbitrator takes the place of a judge, and has many similar powers including, importantly, the right to decide a case and have the decision enforced. It is usual for the arbitration agreement to detail how the arbitrator is selected, for instance by requiring him or her to be a member of the American Arbitration Association. If the two parties cannot agree on the person, the American Arbitration Association may appoint an independent arbitrator for them.

What is essential is that both parties must have agreed in advance that arbitration will be used to settle any dispute, and that is why it should be included in the employee agreement or equivalent document such as an operating agreement for an LLC. It is usual that the arbitrator's judgment cannot be appealed; only sometimes, where it can be shown that the arbitrator has ignored the law, can the judgment be overturned by a court.

There has been some question in the past on whether arbitration agreements are absolutely enforceable, that is, do both parties have to submit to arbitration, or can one party still choose to sue and go to court? It is clear that the arbitration agreements must be well drafted to be enforceable. It is recommended that the agreement contains various checks and measures so that it can be shown to be fair to both sides.

For instance, the agreement cannot limit the award which might be expected if the case went to court. This is not referring simply to the damages claim, but might also include whether the attorneys' fees could be claimed by the winning side. On the other side, the filing fee for arbitration may be more than required to file a lawsuit, and the agreement must provide that the employee will not have to pay more than they would have to if taking the case to court. These provisions are to protect the potentially injured party so that they are not disadvantaged by arbitration compared to the conventional remedy.

Other provisions that must be included to ensure fairness are that the arbitrator must be a neutral party, and that the employer is also bound to settle grievances with his employee by arbitration. The first ensures that the debt is not stacked against the employee by naming a sympathetic or related party as arbitrator; the second provision is required in order for the agreement to be demonstrably fair.

CUSTOMER RELATIONS

The other realm where your employees can harm you and cause you to need your asset protection is in the way they treat your customers, your potential customers, and the way they treat members of the public who they come into contact with during their employment. Sometimes there are frivolous claims of some loss or hurt, and sometimes your staff will perform in an unacceptable way on your behalf.

One of the answers for some of this is to make sure that you provide excellent basic training and ongoing education for your staff. You certainly cannot blame your employees for doing something when they did not know any better, and the areas where you may be at risk should not be expected to be common knowledge. Even if you employ someone who has previously had a similar job in another company, you do not know what work practices they had, or if they were ever trained properly, so you have no excuse for not doing this work.

Your training also needs to cover the scope of the job expected from the employee. If you are negligent in instruction, and the employee suffers an accident on the job, you are likely to be held liable.

Generally, you are likely to be held liable for any negligent act that your employees do while working for your business. This could even apply to an errand that the employee did after work, for instance taking a deposit for the company to a bank and having an accident on the way. You would not be liable if the employee chose to do something illegal, such as drive drunk on this journey, as it plainly was not part of his or her employment to consume alcohol.

You may be wondering if these claims would be covered under your business liability insurance. Many business owners believe that buying a sufficient amount of insurance will protect them from any lawsuit, but this may not be the case. For instance, you may find that your insurance does not cover an intentional act, and it may be held that a wrongful termination, if upheld in court, is an intentional act. That said, as a business owner you would be well advised to buy as wide ranging insurance as you are able to.

18

Combining Businesses to Build a Fortress

"The doorway to success cannot be opened with a key, but rather a combination"
- Daniel Fitzpatrick

In the realm of asset protection combinations of entity are frequently required and used for success. The field is constantly evolving, and you will need to employ specialists to implement any particular strategy that suits your circumstances. They can make sure that the agreements are drafted using the latest case law as a guide to provide the best protections to all you hold dear.

Depending on how complex your affairs are they may recommend that you consider a multi-layered structure, using several entities, and perhaps several types of entity. For extremely wealthy people this is often considered the only way to achieve the security from attack that they desire. It is important to evaluate any such recommendation, and the previous chapters, along with the following chapter which summarizes the business types, will give you the knowledge and the reference material you need to understand why each part of the recommendation is made. You no longer need to just accept your advisers' selections without question, or pay for lengthy sessions so that it can all be explained to you.

David Mandell has written extensively about wealth protection, and is proud of his practice's multi-disciplinary approach.

CASE STUDY: DAVID B. MANDELL

David B. Mandell, JD, MBA, serves as an attorney in the Law Office of David B. Mandell, P.C. and is principal of the consulting firm O'Dell Jarvis Mandell, LLC (**www.ojmgroup.com**).

As a writer, Mandell has co-authored the books *Wealth Secrets: The Keys to Fortune Building and Asset Protection (2008) and WEALTH PROTECTION: Build & Preserve Your Financial Fortress* (2002). Mandell has also written a number of titles specifically for physicians, including *FOR DOCTORS ONLY: A Guide to Working Less & Building More (2007)*, *Wealth Protection, MD* (2004) and *The Doctors Wealth Protection Guide* (1999). He has been interviewed as an expert on over 100 radio programs, as well as Bloomberg and FOX-TV.

Mandell holds a bachelor's degree from Harvard University, where he graduated with honors. His law degree is from the University of California Los Angeles' School of Law, where he was awarded the American Jurisprudence Award for achievement in legal ethics. While at UCLA, Mandell also earned a master's in business administration from the Anderson Graduate School of Management. He can be reached at mandell@ojmgroup.com or 877-656-4362.

In what way are you involved with asset protection, and does this include general estate planning, such as for tax issues?

My work in asset protection began in 1996 when I worked under Arnold S. Goldstein, JD, LLM, PhD, a well-known attorney, author and professor.

CASE STUDY: DAVID B. MANDELL

He was one of the country's experts in the field of asset protection. In 1997, I went out on my own and formed my own law firm and in 1998 formed a consulting firm with a consultant I met at UCLA Anderson business school, Christopher Jarvis. In 2007, our firm became O'Dell Jarvis Mandell, LLC (**www. ojmgroup.com**).

Since our initial days, we have consulted with, and helped, hundreds of physicians, business owners, and families with asset protection planning. We have also delivered hundreds of lectures on the subject to client audiences and fellow advisors, such as attorneys, CPAs, and financial consultants.

While we are not tax or estate planning attorneys ourselves, we have a close network of such counsel in 40 states and pride ourselves on integrating what we do with local counsel. In this way, we are able to service clients effectively nationwide. We presently have over 1,000 clients in 45 states.

Do you specialize in any particular aspects of asset protection, such as foreign trusts or LLCs?

One thing that separates our consulting firm from virtually every other adviser in the field is that we truly consider all options for a client in a multi-disciplinary approach. In our firm, we have attorneys, CPAs, financial planners, MBAs, and, as above, we have relationships with local counsel in 40 states. Thus, we will bring options to the client that might be a legal tool (legal entity such as a trust, LLC, LP or other), exempt retirement plan (defined benefit plan, defined contribution plan, and fringe benefit plan), exempt life insurance or annuity product, use of leverage or financing vehicle, property or casualty insurance arrangement, or other type of solution.

Nearly every attorney will focus their discussion on legal tools — because that is what they understand and providing those tools is how they make a living. That is fine, but is not the entire range of solutions. Often, the more protective, simpler and less costly solution is a financial or insurance tool. On the other hand, legal tools are part of almost every client's planning.

CASE STUDY: DAVID B. MANDELL

Thus, a client should always have a multi-disciplinary coordinated approach to this area of planning – yet is very rare to find this in the marketplace.

In your experience, do you find that a single entity or strategy is sufficient for most people, or do you commonly recommend a multi-layered structure?

I think it completely depends on the circumstances. Factors include: what type of entity, how is it created and drafted, what state are the clients in, what is the state of the law regarding that type of entity in that state, what type of other techniques to protect the asset could be used instead of or along with the legal entity. If the client can move equity into a state exempt asset, that might be a lot easier, cost efficient, and more protective than even a multi-entity arrangement. We have seen this work well for many clients.

Have you found that you have needed to change your methods in recent years, because of FTC v. Affordable Media, or to include Nevis LLCs?

In our practice, we lay out the option of international planning for the appropriate clients — and we can refer those who want to move forward to attorneys who have experience in setting up these arrangements. However, in our experience, relatively few clients will take on the expense, tax reporting requirements, and general maintenance of these arrangements. Some of the attorneys we work with have become more wary of international planning in recent years and others continue to have confidence in it. We leave that judgment to the attorneys who work in the area day to day.

Briefly describe a "success" story, that is, an asset protection plan that was threatened in some way and withstood the attack, and why. Please change names as you think fit.

A physician came to us close to five years ago and we recommended a number of steps in their plan. We created a significantly defined benefit plan in the practice and they also invested each month into a cash accumulation life insurance policy, as part of their wealth accumulation plan.

CASE STUDY: DAVID B. MANDELL

In addition, we referred them to a local attorney who created an LLC for other assets they owned.

Two years ago, they were successfully sued in a malpractice action. The judgment went beyond their coverage limits and they had to negotiate with the judgment creditor. Both the retirement plan and life policy cash values were 100 percent protected and they were able to settle with the creditor for a relatively small amount for the LLC-owned assets. The clients were relieved and thankful.

Briefly describe an unsuccessful story where assets were seized — this may well be the story of someone who came to you for advice after the lawsuit. Please change names as you think fit.

Because of our exposure as nationally-known experts and authors, we often have potential clients contacting us after they have an event of duress or even during litigation. We are very careful of the type of clients we take on. Nonetheless, we often have clients who — because of their field — are always involved in some type of litigation. We explain to them that the planning we recommend will be effective as to future unforeseen claims, but not what is facing them presently.

If relevant, what changes did you recommend to improve the asset protection in this last case?

To use the present threats as a "wake up call" and protect assets against future now unforeseen claims.

It is worth repeating a warning that has been running as a theme through the preceding chapters — you have to be committed to maintaining the structure and running all the businesses correctly, including holding meetings and taking minutes, filing returns with the state, and keeping separate accounts, if you do not want it all to be in vain. There is no point in going to the trouble of a complicated structure if the first challenge can pierce the veil and take your assets.

The alternative may be to adopt a simple but capable structure that will give you good protections, and that you can maintain. This chapter reviews several multi business structures and discuss their advantages.

One of the most important questions is whether you own rental or investment real estate. It is almost always a mistake to hold real estate in the same business entity as other assets. Real estate presents its own particular risks, and if other assets are in the same company then they can be attacked at the same time. You have the potential for significant exposure from real estate when you consider all the things that can happen, and you do not want to make a gift to a creditor of other assets when they sue.

RETAIL BUSINESS

If you have your own business, which has a storefront or office, this is another case where you should consider a separate entity from the business operation for holding the real estate. For instance, perhaps you have a business selling surfboards, and you also own the building that you operate in. Although you may have regarded this as a single business until now, there can be asset protection and tax advantages in splitting up the operations.

Selling surfboards produces income that would be considered earned income for tax purposes. As such, in the simplest form of business, a sole proprietorship, the total income would be subject to self employment tax, as well as other applicable taxes. There would be no asset protection in this form of business. A general partnership would also pay the self employment tax, and provides no asset protection.

If you chose to use a limited partnership, it would give asset protection to the limited partners, who would also not be subject to self employment tax. Remember though that limited partners cannot work in the business or make management decisions, and that would mean using this entity in this case would make no sense.

The LLC is a popular form of business entity nowadays. It would provide you with the asset protection which the previous ones do not. However, you will still have to pay the self employment tax on all the earned income, making the LLC only part of the answer. For a better solution, you should consider the corporate entities.

The C-Corporation will give you the asset protection that you need. However, it does attract corporate taxation at 15 percent before you even get to pay yourself. While there are some deductions for business expenses that you can take with a C-Corporation, on balance in this situation it may not be the best.

The best for this application is probably the S-corporation. But remember that every situation is different. You must work with your advisers to evaluate how different entities will work out for you, to calculate your profit projections and expenses, and to take into account the other factors such as asset protection. This will tell you whether you will maintain the company filing formalities. However, the S-Corporation is favored in many of these circumstances.

The S-Corporation gives you the asset protection that you need, and that you are reading this book to find out about. The advantages for the S-Corporation are firstly that it is a pass-through tax entity, and you will not pay corporate tax. Secondly, it can be used to reduce the self-employment tax that you would pay on the whole amount of the earned income with the LLC. You can do this by taking a reasonable salary, as discussed in the chapter on corporations, and as long as you are not too greedy, you should have no problem taking the rest of the earned income without paying self employment tax on it. The amount in excess of a reasonable salary would be considered a distribution of profits.

So far, your consideration has not been very different from the discussions in the previous chapters. But the train of thought that you need to follow to form an overall plan requires you to consider each section of your work and assets. Diversifying your assets over several entities is one of the options to make seizure more difficult for any creditor, and means that if any one fails, by piercing the veil or other court decision, the creditor does not automatically get access to all your assets.

While S-Corporations may be suitable for enterprises that have earned income, they are not always as useful for owning real estate, so if you decide to separate the building that houses the business from the sales side, you will want to consider all the types of entities again. This is an opportunity to organize your overall activities for your benefit, so you should seriously consider forming a separate entity; the idea would be that the sales operation would pay rent to the real estate entity, just as if you were renting the building from an outsider. The income that the real estate company receives would be passive income, so would not be subject to self employment tax, and the rent would be deductible to the sales operation.

Considering again a sole proprietorship, a general partnership, or a limited partnership, you will find that they do not have the previous problem of taxation for self employment tax on the income because the rent is considered passive income. But, they do have asset protection issues as previously discussed, and the limited partner can run into the problem of having no activity or management allowed. Thus, these are not the best choice.

The C-Corporation suffers from the same drawbacks as before, in that it is not a pass through entity and corporate tax has to be paid on the profits before they are even given to you, when you will be taxed again. As your corporation cannot simply pay you passive income, the money that you take from the rental activity would be classified as unearned income and you would pay income tax on top of the corporate tax. In fact, you have discovered a way to transform passive income into earned income, which is a disadvantage. You do, however, have the asset protection that you need.

As mentioned above, the S-corporation may also not be considered the best vehicle to cover the rental activity. It is true that you get asset protection with this form of business entity, which is an advantage over the partnership arrangements. You will recall that in the retailing operation where we chose the S-corporation the earned income is subject to self employment tax, but you are able to declare how much of the income is earned, and take the rest as profits, therefore saving some tax. For a rental business the income is passive, so there is no advantage to be had from the S-corporation.

This leads us to the LLC, which again protects your assets as the corporations do. The disadvantage with the LLC for the retailing operation was that self-employment tax must be paid on all earned income. As the rental income is passive income, the LLC is not liable to self employment tax, and would be a good choice in these circumstances.

This is just one of the ways that you can combine business entities to your advantage. It is a simple example, but the idea is powerful. Your retail business simply enters into a standard lease agreement with the LLC to use the property. If anyone sues your retail business, your real estate will not be subject to seizure, as it is owned by a totally separate entity.

MEDICAL PRACTICE

Suppose now we consider the position of a medical practice. This would be the sort of occupation which is particularly concerned with being sued. The strategy outlined above under retail practice could be used, or the doctors involved could form a limited partnership, and the choice is something that they would each need to discuss with an adviser to determine that its use fits their circumstances. There is an important addition, though.

Medical equipment is often very expensive, and worth protecting from the reach of a creditor. In this case, you may want to look thoughtfully at having a separate business entity that owns the equipment and that rents it to the doctors in the practice.

CONSTRUCTION COMPANY

You can use the same sort of thinking in any business where you have expensive equipment that you would like to hold separately to keep it away from possible creditors. For instance, a construction company may need bulldozers, concrete mixers, etc. The machinery which is high dollar can be better protected from seizure by having it rented to the building company, so that if there is a liability case, the machinery will be kept intact and possibly another building company can be started or the equipment sold if the original company has to fold.

The basic idea is that the building company does the work and is the risky business. Yet it owns very little that can be seized. The LLC or corporation that owns the equipment has all the equity, but does nothing with it that can put it at risk of a lawsuit.

You should not take this example as a model that you should follow under all circumstances, however. There are many ways to plan your asset protection and tax reductions, and your particular circumstances should be taken into account when considering the pros and cons of each method.

For instance, in the above example your building company may have several employees. While the S-corporation was a good choice in the retail example, in this case you may want to consider the C-corporation. Such a choice would be good if you wanted to offer your employees benefits like medical insurance. The premiums for this would be tax deductible. As the business is able to afford it, you can offer all the other benefits that big corporations include, and this will help you with staff retention. One of the best benefits that you can provide for yourself and your employees is a retirement plan. You might also consider other fringe benefits, such as an education allowance and a company car. Finally, you may even consider rewarding your employees with a share ownership plan. All of these things are facilitated by having a C-corporation.

When you come to consider other assets that you have, you may well find that you need more business entities to maximize your protection.

As many people do, you may have accumulated a couple of rental properties. Perhaps you have nearly paid off the loans on them, which leaves you with a great deal of equity exposed for a creditor to target. A claim could come from an accident occurring on these properties, or from another direction when the creditor would seek to take whatever assets of yours are available.

Obviously, these properties should be held in a business structure which provides asset protection. You may be tempted to use a limited partnership or an LLC to hold both of them, and this would not be a bad plan, but it would be better to use a separate entity for each. That way, if one of the properties has a claim, the creditor cannot reach the other property as settlement. If the properties are jointly owned by one company, there is no obstacle to them both being seized.

It may seem to you that creating and maintaining several LLCs so that each rental property may be separately owned is more work and more cost than you are prepared to incur. This is somewhat of a dilemma, and consequently, with the evolving nature of the asset protection, several states have come out with statutes that facilitate what are called Series LLCs.

So far, the seven states that have passed such laws are Delaware, Illinois, Iowa, Nevada, Oklahoma, Tennessee, and Utah. The idea of the Series LLC is that it can amend its operating agreement to establish other LLCs within the original LLC. The immediate benefit is that this cuts down on costs as you are only filing for one company while maintaining separate asset protection entities.

The key to this is that each LLC contained within the original one can have its own property, assets, and business purpose, and the debts and liabilities of that LLC can only be enforced against its own assets, and not against any of the other related LLCs. Thus, you have the benefits of totally separate Limited Liability Companies without so much paperwork.

In fact, some of the states have included extra features compared to a standard LLC. These include protection from claims that are not caused by the actions of the LLC, for instance personal liability perhaps from a traffic accident. The LLC can serve to protect the assets of the owner from being claimed to satisfy such a burden.

While these are very desirable features, you should note that you may have a problem in certain circumstances trying to use a Series LLC if you do not reside in one of the states that recognizes it. In the end, it will come down to your state of residence to decide how they would like to treat such an outside entity in which they have no established case law. At the least, you may find that they wish to charge you taxes as they would for individual LLCs. Once again, this is where your team of advisers will be invaluable in advising how your state has and is likely to view such an entity.

ICE CREAM PARLOR

This is an example of a different way to approach asset protection. A husband and wife have an ice cream parlor as a family business. They consider the possibilities, and decide that they would prefer to use a limited partnership to own the business. The reason that they decide to do this is that they wish to have a means to gradually shift the value of the business to their children, and see that this is an entity in which their children can be limited partners, and can be gifted shares in the company gradually. The general partner will still retain all control over the operation of the business regardless of the amount of the children's shares.

As discussed in the limited partnership chapter, the general partner in a limited partnership is responsible for all liabilities, and is a risky position for any individual to occupy. However, the general partner can be a corporation or LLC which have asset protection advantages. In this case, they decide to use an LLC as the general partner.

In setting up the companies, they decide that the LLC will hold a four percent interest in the limited partnership as general partner. Note that it is not necessary that the general partner in a limited partnership has any particular share of the partnership, and in this case, the general partner wants to have most of the value distributed in the family ownership, amongst the limited partners. The husband and wife are limited partners, each holding a 48 percent interest. The plan is that they can gift part of their shares to their children year by year, in an amount that does not exceed the gift tax allowances, and they will work towards each limited partner holding 24 percent in the partnership.

This leaves the question of how the LLC will be formed. As the husband and wife are open to being sued in the course of their business, it would not work for them to be in the financial majority control of the LLC. The LLC is the general partner of the business, and thus controls the limited partnership. If the husband and wife are majority owners of the LLC, they can be forced by court order to make distributions from the limited partnership to respond to a lawsuit. This does not prohibit them taking management positions, such as president or CEO in the LLC, but they do not want to be the ultimate owners.

They get around this by making their adult children the majority owners, trusting that they will do the right thing if the assets are threatened. As the LLC only owns 4 percent of the limited partnership, the value of this majority ownership does not exceed the gift tax allowance.

Consider what happens if the husband or wife is sued. The assets are 24 percent each in the limited partnership, but the creditor cannot touch these because of the limited liability. All the creditor can do is obtain a charging order against any profits or distributions from the partnership. The distributions from the partnership will be decided by the general partner, who is the LLC, and it is likely that no actual distributions will be made because of the charging order.

Furthermore, profits can be allocated by filing with the IRS, and these would fall into the realm of phantom income which would require the creditor to pay taxes on money that he had not received. With this powerful disincentive to pursuing full settlement, it is likely that the creditor will settle for a much reduced amount.

We have just started considering the various structures that can be set up to provide asset protection, and each case is different. You will sometimes have companies that are each owned in some way by an individual, or, as in this latter case, you will sometimes have companies with an ownership interest in another company, making a multi-layered entity. These structures can become very complex, expensive to set up, and costly to maintain. In consultation with your financial advisers you will be able to consider a cost benefit analysis and decide at what level you feel adequately protected.

In your considerations, you must be careful to identify both the inside liabilities and the outside liabilities, and how they will be treated for any particular structure. The inside liabilities are those which come from the company's operations. For example, you may serve ice cream that makes someone seriously ill. The idea of using a corporation, LLC, or limited partnership is that you personally are protected from the liability created by your company. In this respect, all these entities are equivalent, provided that there is no argument for piercing the veil.

Outside liabilities, on the other hand, do not result from the company's operations. For instance, a personal car accident might result in being sued. You need to test your asset protection structure to ensure that, as far as possible, the person suing cannot seize the assets of your business in settlement. If you arrange your affairs in good order, the most that a creditor can get from your business will be a charging order for future dividend distributions which, as we noted above, can be discretionary requiring the creditor to pay tax on money that he has not received. As the statutes governing LLCs can vary from state to state, the most universal entity to ensure charging order remedies is a limited partnership, and you should seek expert advice for your circumstance. The court may choose to decide on the sufficiency of the charging order by taking into account whether the limited partnership is a valid business or is just formed to avoid loss of the assets. The court may also look to see if there are other innocent partners who would be harmed by the partnership assets being fixed; the court may decide that the assets can be forfeited if it perceives a structure with no purpose but to frustrate creditors.

Summary

Asset protection can be considered an essential in modern society, and this book covered the different aspects that you should consider. There are many facts and ideas presented, and you may be wondering how to proceed. Here is a summary of the basic points on which you should focus your attention:

- To protect your assets, you must make them inaccessible. The general principle is that if you can get at them, then you can be ordered by a court to give them to the creditor, or stand in contempt and go to jail if you do not. You can make them inaccessible using various entities, or by equity stripping.

- In your business, it is good to separate your physical assets from your money making. The physical assets should be in one entity that takes no risks but leases the equipment and real estate to the income generating side, which is exposed to risk.

- In your personal life, it is good to separate your dangerous assets, which might cause a claim, from your safe assets, such as shares, in any asset protection strategy.

- If you have rental property, you may hold several in the same entity, but are better advised to have a separate LP or LLC for each property, otherwise an accident on one can seize all of your real estate assets in the company.

- You must maintain the formalities of meetings, filings, and accounts for each entity in order for it not to be set aside by the court.

- Avoid general partnerships.

- Do not give a personal guarantee.

- Do not buy a packaged solution from a seminar.

A Family Limited Partnership has significant advantages that provide asset protection and taxable estate reduction by gifting shares to your children. A living trust with a pour-over will avoid passing your assets through probate.

Everybody's situation is different, both in the assets owned and your future plans. You should use experts in the asset protection field to discuss, decide on, and set up the structure that suits your circumstances, making sure that the latest legal advice is taken into account. The information that is contained in this book will enable you to minimize the time that you need to spend with your advisers and thus their cost. With the background of knowledge that you have from this book, you will quickly be able to see the reasons for any recommendations.

Business Types Compared

The various types of entity under which you can run your business are explained in the previous chapters, and this section provides a comparison table to assist in your understanding.

In looking at all of these company formations, you must bear in mind that the more complicated the structure you create, the more committed you must be to maintain it. They are useless if the litigant can pierce the veil, and show that the company was a sham designed purely for asset protection. In fact, if you think you have protection and you do not, then they are worse than useless.

In considering how serious the threat is to your assets, you will have to make a judgment which will take in all aspects of your life, and particularly what type of employment you are in, and whether you own your own business. While no one can guarantee that you will or will not get sued, obviously some lines of work are more vulnerable to attack. It would be ideal to have a strategy which was bullet proof against any attack, and some schemes come close to this; but there is always a chance that a determined and well financed opponent will penetrate the defenses. Diversification of assets and making it difficult, firstly for the assets to be identified, and secondly for the assets to be seized, is realistically the best defense to dissuade potential creditors from pursuing you too vigorously.

The entities are listed in the order discussed previously. The corporations can continue forever, subject to keeping the filing processes up-to-date. The other entities exist only while their members or shareholders do. Most of the business entities are fairly flexible in application, with the S- and C-corporations being the least flexible.

You are always best advised to get it in writing, and this includes any agreements that you have with other people, particularly other investors in the company, and any statutory meetings and other paperwork. This advice applies regardless of if you are legally required to do so.

While taxation is another aspect that you will need to keep in mind when deciding on your company formation, because of the potentially large effect of this decision on your payments, you may also need to consider the extent of deductions that you can receive with some formations, which may include services such as health insurance. Certainly, this aspect needs to be balanced with other factors, such as the ability to obtain commercial finance, should your business require it. The first two formations will be the most difficult to finance, with the sole proprietorship probably requiring a personal guarantee, and the C-corporation is perhaps the easiest to raise money for.

	Ownership	Liability	Tax	Formalities
Sole Proprietorship	One owner	Unlimited	Pass through to owner	None required
General Partnership	Any number and type of general partners (at least two)	Unlimited	Pass through to general partners	None required, but partnership agreement recommended
Limited Partnership	Any number and type of owners – at least one general partner, at least one limited partner	Unlimited for general partner(s) – limited for limited partners	Pass through to both types of partner	File with state. Agreement and annual meeting not required but recommended
Limited Liability Company	Any number and type of owners – called members	Generally no personal liability for members	Pass through to members (unless they elect otherwise)	File with state. Agreement and annual meeting not required but recommended
S Corporation	Up to 75 shareholders – all to be US citizens	Generally no personal liability for shareholders	Pass through to shareholders	File with state. Bylaws and annual meetings required
C Corporation	Any number of shareholders	Generally no personal liability for shareholders	Corporation taxed, and shareholders taxed on dividends	File with state. Bylaws and annual meetings required

APPENDIX B

State Specific Factors

Here the homestead and retirement plan exemptions are detailed by state. This is of necessity a summary of the available reliefs, and if the item is important to your asset planning, you must go over the actual legal provisions with your advisers.

In many cases the homestead exemption depends on the size of the homestead, and there may be other qualifications in the statutes.

The retirement exemptions can vary for teachers, government employees, judges, and firefighters. You should confirm the details with the statute, as information may change after publication of this book.

	SINGLE HOMESTEAD EXEMPTION	MARRIED HOMESTEAD EXEMPTION	RETIREMENT PLAN
Alabama	$5,000	$10,000	Non-ERISA plans protected
Alaska	$67,500	$67,500	Non-ERISA plans protected up to $12,500 of the unmatured value
Arizona	$150,000	$150,000	Non-ERISA plans protected

	SINGLE HOMESTEAD EXEMPTION	MARRIED HOMESTEAD EXEMPTION	RETIREMENT PLAN
Arkansas	$2,500	$2,500	Non-ERISA plans protected
California	$50,000	$75,000	Non-ERISA plans protected
Colorado	$45,000	$45,000	Non-ERISA plans protected
Connecticut	$75,000	$75,000	Non-ERISA plans protected
Delaware	None	None	Non-ERISA plans protected
District of Columbia	None	None	Non-ERISA plans protected
Florida	Unlimited	Unlimited	Non-ERISA plans protected
Georgia	$5,000	$5,000	Non-ERISA plans protected
Hawaii	$20,000	$30,000	Non-ERISA plans protected
Idaho	$50,000	$50,000	Non-ERISA plans protected
Illinois	$7,500	$15,000	Non-ERISA plans protected
Indiana	$7,500	$7,500	Non-ERISA plans protected
Iowa	Unlimited	Unlimited	Only ERISA plans protected
Kansas	Unlimited	Unlimited	Non-ERISA plans protected
Kentucky	$5,000	$5,000	Non-ERISA plans protected
Louisiana	$25,000	$25,000	Non-ERISA plans protected
Maine	$35,000	$70,000	Non-ERISA plans protected up to $15,000

	SINGLE HOMESTEAD EXEMPTION	MARRIED HOMESTEAD EXEMPTION	RETIREMENT PLAN
Maryland	None	None	Non-ERISA plans protected
Massachusetts	$500,000	$500,000	Non-ERISA plans protected with some limitations
Michigan	$3,500	$3,500	Non-ERISA plans protected
Minnesota	$200,000	$200,000	Non-ERISA plans protected up to $60,000 total
Mississippi	$75,000	$75,000	Non-ERISA plans protected
Missouri	$15,000	$15,000	Non-ERISA plans protected
Montana	$100,000	$100,000	Non-ERISA plans protected with some limitations
Nebraska	$12,500	$12,500	Non-ERISA plans protected
Nevada	$550,000	$550,000	Non-ERISA plans protected up to $500,000 total
New Hampshire	$100,000	$200,000	Non-ERISA plans protected if set up after 1998
New Jersey	None	None	Non-ERISA plans protected
New Mexico	$30,000	$60,000	No distinction between ERISA and standard plans
New York	$10,000	$20,000	Non-ERISA plans protected
North Carolina	$10.000	$20,000	Non-ERISA plans protected
North Dakota	$80,000	$80,000	Non-ERISA plans protected up to $200,000 total

	SINGLE HOMESTEAD EXEMPTION	MARRIED HOMESTEAD EXEMPTION	RETIREMENT PLAN
Ohio	$5,000	$10,000	Non-ERISA plans protected
Oklahoma	Unlimited	Unlimited	Non-ERISA plans protected
Oregon	$25,000	$33,000	Non-ERISA plans protected
Pennsylvania	None	None	Non-ERISA plans protected
Rhode Island	None	None	Non-ERISA plans protected
South Carolina	$5,000	$10,000	Non-ERISA plans protected
South Dakota	$30,000 ($170,000 for seniors)	$30,000 ($170,000 for seniors)	Non-ERISA plans protected up to $250,000 total
Tennessee	$5,000	$7,500	Non-ERISA plans protected
Texas	Unlimited	Unlimited	Non-ERISA plans protected
Utah	$20,000	$40,000	Non-ERISA plans protected
Vermont	$75,000	$75,000	Non-ERISA plans protected
Virginia	$5,000	$10,000	Non-ERISA plans protected up to a total that would yield $25,000 annually
Washington	$40,000	$40,000	Non-ERISA plans protected
West Virginia	$25,000	$25,000	Non-ERISA plans protected
Wisconsin	$40,000	$40,000	Non-ERISA plans protected
Wyoming	$10,000	$20,000	Non-ERISA plans protected

APPENDIX

C Assets Checklist

To assist in formulating your plan, here is a list that you can use to more clearly evaluate what your significant asset exposures are.

ASSET	FAIR MARKET VALUE $	LIENS $	EXEMP-TION $	NET WORTH $	HOW TITLED $
Personal					
Home					
Vehicles					
Stocks and shares					
Bank accounts, and CDs					

ASSET	FAIR MARKET VALUE $	LIENS $	EXEMP- TION $	NET WORTH $	HOW TITLED $
Commodities such as gold or other precious metals owned					
Personal property					
Retirement and benefits - Pensions, Individual Retire- ment Accounts (IRAs), simplified employee pension plans					
Life insurance cash value/face value					
Long-term care insur- ance					
Other items					
Business					
Furniture and office furnishing					

ASSET	FAIR MARKET VALUE $	LIENS $	EXEMP-TION $	NET WORTH $	HOW TITLED $
Current assets — accounts and notes receivable					
Tools of the trade, inventory					
Ownership interests, limited partnerships, unrealized investments					
Other items					

APPENDIX

D

Glossary

Administrator: someone who administers a will.

Appeal: the process to challenge a court's decision.

Attachment: a way of collecting a judgment by levying on property held by a third party.

Beneficiary: a person who benefits from a trust, or from a will.

Community property: property is assumed to be held jointly by both spouses in a community property jurisdiction.

Corporation: a business formed according to legal requirements, see the relevant chapter for full description.

Creditor: a person or organization that has a legal claim on others' property or money.

Default: when a debtor does not fulfill the contract, typically by not making a payment.

Default judgment: a judgment made when the defendant does not respond to the charge.

Defendant: the person required to answer a legal complaint, or who has been charged with a crime.

Deposition: evidence given under oath before the proceedings.

Distribution: a division of profits from a company.

Donor: a person who makes a gift.

Double taxation: arises when a corporation pays taxes on profits and shareholders pay taxes again on the distribution of the profits as dividends. See chapter on corporations.

ERISA: the Employee Retirement Income Security Act, which is a Federal statute establishing standards for pension plans.

Estate tax: a tax that may be due on the death of a taxpayer, depending on the amount of his or her possessions, and their disposition.

Executor: a person named in the will to be an administrator.

Fair market value: what property may be readily sold for, given a free market and no compulsion on buyer or seller.

Family limited partnership: a limited partnership owned by a family.

Foreclosure: the legal proceeding by which a party, usually the bank, repossesses property held as security against a debt which has been defaulted on.

Fraudulent conveyance: the transferring of funds to evade paying a creditor, usually by donating to a friend.

Fraudulent transfer: same as fraudulent conveyance.

Garnishment: deducting money from your paycheck before you get it, by court order to your employer.

General partner: an owner of a partnership who can be held liable for all debts, and usually has a management role.

General partnership: a partnership with only general partners, the common form of partnership requiring no particular formalities to set up. See relevant chapter.

Gift: for taxation purposes, transferring property without receiving value in exchange.

Gift tax: a tax due if the value of a gift exceeds limits.

Grantor: the person who establishes and funds a trust.

Homestead exemption: a legal protection intended to protect you from losing your home,

but varies from state to state and can be of little value.

Inter vivos trust: a trust established during a person's lifetime, also called a living trust.

Irrevocable: usually referring to a trust, this means it cannot be changed, which is important to have assets removed from your control.

Joint tenancy: a legal form of owning a house where the joint owners have each a right to the whole house on the death of the other.

Judgment creditor: a creditor who has received a judgment from a court.

Liability: responsibility for a loss or damage, usually associated with having to provide restitution.

Lien: a form of security interest held over property, usually in return for debt and restricting the sale of the property.

Limited liability: used about a business entity, which can be sued in itself, but the owners cannot be held accountable for it. Their liability is limited.

Limited liability company (LLC): an entity formed under a statute, see relevant chapter for details.

Limited partner: an owner in a limited partnership who cannot participate in management and has no personal liability for the partnership's debts.

Limited partnership: a partnership that has at least one general partner and as many limited partners as required.

Manager: runs an LLC, but does not have to be a member.

Member: an owner of an LLC, similar to a shareholder in a corporation.

Operating agreement: a contract between owners of an LLC, spelling out rights and responsibilities, what to do on death of a member, etc.

Pass-through tax status: for certain business entities, where the profits and losses of the business pass through as though the business did not exist, and are reported on personal tax returns.

Plaintiff: someone who brings a lawsuit against a defendant.

Pour-over will: a will that is used to transfer property to a living trust on death. This accounts for items which were not included in the living trust during life, or were acquired after the trust was funded.

Revocable: usually referring to a trust, this can be changed by the grantor after it is formed.

S-corporation: a business entity whose income is usually passed through to be taxed at the shareholder level.

Self settled trust: a trust where the settlor is the same as the beneficiary. Usually not a viable trust for asset protection.

Settlor: same as grantor.

Shareholders: owners of a corporation.

Sole proprietorship: a business with one owner (or with a spouse), this is the default entity when operating a business.

Supremacy clause: in the United States Constitution, this establishes that Federal statutes are "the supreme law of the land". This means that if state laws conflict with it, Federal law trumps them.

Tenancy by the entirety: a way to hold real estate in some states, available only to married couples.

Trust: a legal document that instructs a trustee to manage property for the grantor.

Bibliography

Financing Accounts Receivable for Retirement and Asset Protection

   Ronald J. Adkisson

Asset Protection 101 – Tax and Legal Strategies of the Rich

   J. J. Childers

So Sue Me! – How to Protect Your Assets from the Lawsuit Explosion

   Arnold S. Goldstein

Wealth Secrets of the Affluent – Keys to Fortune Building and Asset Protection

   Christopher R. Jarvis and David B. Mandell

Asset Protection – Protect Your Wealth, Limit Your Exposure to Lawsuits, Maximize Your Tax Savings

   Robert F. Klueger

Lawyers Are Liars – The Truth About Protecting Our Assets!

Mark J. Kohler

Rich Dad's Real Estate Advantages – Tax and Legal Secrets of Successful Real Estate Investors

Sharon Lechter and Garrett Sutton

How to Use Limited Liability Companies & Limited Partnerships – Getting the Most Out of Your Legal Structure

Garrett Sutton

Author
Biography

Alan Northcott is an author, freelance writer, trader, engineer and farmer, along with other pursuits, and he now lives in the Mid-West. Originating from England, he immigrated with his wife to America in 1992. His engineering career spanned more than 30 years, on both sides of the Atlantic, and recent years have found him seeking and living a more diverse and fulfilling lifestyle. He has other financial books out and in the works, and offers a free newsletter on various related topics. You can find out more at **www.alannorthcott.com**, or e-mail him directly at alannorthcott@msn.com.

Index

C

Community property, 273, 70, 198-204, 216

Corporation, 263, 273-274, 276-277, 61, 63, 80, 86-88, 92-99, 101, 111, 156, 158, 175-176, 178, 189, 214-216, 225, 249, 251, 254, 257, 20, 7, 9, 397-409, 16, 32, 74-75, 159, 162-163, 257-263, 425, 429

Creditor, 273-275, 31-33, 38, 41, 54-60, 63-65, 70-71, 73-74, 76-77, 84, 87-90, 120-123, 126, 134, 138-139, 153, 157-158, 160-161, 164, 168, 173-174, 178-179, 182-184, 187, 190, 195-197, 199, 211, 216-217, 221-223, 225-226, 245-246, 248, 251-252, 256-257, 259, 22, 14

D

Default, 273, 277, 82, 85, 198, 206, 220, 222, 10, 13, 121, 263

Default judgment, 273

Defendant, 273-274, 276

Deposition, 274

Distribution, 274, 90, 112, 138, 161, 178, 206, 208, 248, 49, 247

Donor, 274, 410, 32, 52, 68, 74-75, 79, 89, 97, 106, 117, 134, 143, 179-180, 215-217, 220, 222-223, 225-228, 230-233, 243, 250, 254, 272-273, 276, 290, 294, 296-297, 299, 326, 347-348, 359, 370-371, 376, 386, 418, 421, 423, 425, 432, 8, 12

Double taxation, 274, 97-98, 102

E

Employee identification number, 81

ERISA, 266-267, 274, 33, 69, 71-72

Estate tax, 274, 106, 114, 135-136, 140, 147, 167, 206-209, 20

Executor, 274, 206, 208

J

Joint tenancy, 275

Judgment creditor, 275, 158, 245

L

Liability, 263, 280, 275-276, 30, 34, 38, 40, 44-45, 47, 86-88, 92-94, 99-103, 111, 113-117, 120, 176-178, 180, 188-189, 199-200, 202, 216, 228-229, 231, 240, 251, 253, 256-257, 21, 2, 7, 10-11, 13-14, 70, 79, 82-85, 214, 269, 325, 358, 427, 2

Lien, 275, 32, 120, 168, 196, 222-224, 226

Limited liability, 263, 280, 276, 38, 93-94, 101, 103, 116-117, 176, 188-189, 216, 253, 256, 21, 7, 10, 14

Limited liability company (LLC), 276

Limited partner, 263, 276, 88-91, 249, 255

Limited partnership, 263, 274, 276, 60, 62, 80, 86-89, 91-92, 102-103, 187-188, 247, 249-250, 252, 254-257, 260, 21, 7, 9

M

Manager, 276, 72, 103, 106, 108, 112, 177-179, 412-414, 78, 280, 290-292, 301, 343, 349, 386, 424, 2

Member, 276, 48, 55, 103-104, 108, 112, 115-117, 140, 157, 166, 178-179, 189-190, 216, 219, 223, 238, 402, 405-407, 19, 30, 38, 42, 44-45, 47-50, 60, 62-65, 72-73, 79, 89, 98, 103, 105, 135, 141, 149, 160, 178, 205, 219, 239, 247, 270, 291-292, 326, 328, 331, 336, 343, 348, 356, 358, 360, 374, 376, 386, 393, 421, 424-425, 434

O

Operating agreement, 276, 61, 107, 117, 238, 253